ordinary MIRACLES

*Snapshots of a life
and ministry
to encourage you
on the way*

ROB COYLE

a. Acorn Press

Published by Acorn Press
An imprint of Bible Society Australia
ACN 148 058 306 | Charity licence 19 000 528
GPO Box 4161
Sydney NSW 2001
Australia
www.acornpress.net.au | www.biblesociety.org.au

ISBN 978-0-647-53332-1

First published by Morning Star Publishing in 2020, ISBN 978-0-647-53074-0

NATIONAL
LIBRARY
OF AUSTRALIA
A catalogue record for this work is available from the National Library of Australia

Cover and text design and layout by John Healy

Eugene Peterson extolls the virtue of a long obedience in the same direction. However, while rare in a world of instant gratification, all great servants of Christ discover the power of modelling genuine discipleship over a lifetime.

One such pilgrim is Rob Coyle. Over a lifetime, he has become a spiritual father to hundreds, myself included. Over a lifetime, he has continually demonstrated the power of prayer, not only amidst crises, but in his quiet walk alongside his God. Over a lifetime, he has found his God entirely faithful and preached this faithfulness to many thousands of people, both young and old.

Over three decades leading Youth Dimension, he created a space for young people to learn about God's kindness and power, facilitating many into a relationship with our creator and vocational ministry.

He loves his Lord; he loves his family and adores the church. Ordinary Miracles *honours a lifetime of faithful service in evangelism and discipleship. It contains a rare opportunity for 'a look under the bonnet' to reveal the innervations and inner workings of one of Australia's most influential men and organisations for the gospel of Christ.*

Dr Lindsay Tunbridge
CEO Youth Dimensison.

It's probably fair to say that Rob Coyle is one of the most effective developers of Christian leadership that I know. Some years ago I wrote an essay on leadership development, and in my research it became abundantly clear that Rob's leadership development processes were world class. By observation, this was not intentional. By following Jesus ruthlessly in his own life, mission and family, and by teaching others to do the same, Rob Coyle seems to have accidently become what Jim Collins calls a level five leader*. There is no doubt that I will be indebted to Rob for the rest of my days in his exemplifying the leadership of vocational, family and internal life.

Chris Danes
Senior Pastor Syndal Baptist

*Jim Collins; Good to Great

As a former intern and staff member at Youth Dimension, there were a number of occasions when the concept of Rob writing a book came up. The affirmation for this concept from my perspective was based on Rob's impact on me as an individual.

I came to faith under Rob's ministry in high schools. He co-officiated at my wedding to my wife. He invested into me personally over 6 years as an intern and staff member at YD.

My excitement about his book stems from those days; the profound wisdom, insight, Godly perspective and life change that has come from sitting under Rob's leadership. Rob Coyle has been, without doubt, the single most influential person in my spiritual formation, and so it is my hope that Ordinary Miracles *will open that up to thousands of others. There is absolutely no way I would be in ministry now, (25 years on) without Rob's investment. May God bless you with Rob's insight and experience.*

Steve Peach
Senior Pastor Southport Baptist.

*I dedicate this book to the rock of my life, my wife Pam,
who knows the worst of me and still has loved me,
giving me a taste of the unconditional love of Jesus.*

CONTENTS

Before You Start

It's a paralysing feeling, sensing you're about to get murdered. Like a glacier sliding down my spine, it froze me. Is it a miracle I survived?

Staff with house mortgages, many mouths to feed and a ministry to run. Where was the money to come from? We needed a miracle.

A seven-year-old grandchild on death's door. Would God step in and do a miracle?

Nine years working in schools sharing the gospel by myself, and I felt as lonely as a vegetarian at a BBQ. It would take a miracle to keep me going.

Miracles can be more than resurrections, amazing healings and revivals. They can be what I call 'ordinary miracles'. This is a record of such events.

One of my favourite ways to entertain the grandkids in the car and stop them from fighting is to play a particular game. They still haven't grown tired of it. First, I give them a lolly. This is always a winner. Second, I explain the rules of the game: you must suck the lolly, not bite it, and the one who keeps the lolly the longest in the mouth is the winner.

What you are about to read are moments in my life and ministry that I have sucked on. You will notice that I often draw out some principle of life, discipleship and leadership that I have rolled around on my tongue like a lollipop. And I want you to savour these moments with me.

In a world where change is rapid and yesterday is old news, I have had the privilege to work in outreach and discipleship for over forty-three years. A lot has changed in that time.

I initially trained to be a primary teacher and teacher of the deaf. I taught for three years, then my wife Pam and I spent three years at the Melbourne Bible Institute (MBI). From here, I worked with Victoria Open Air Campaigners (OAC) from 1971 to 1978, at its height of impact. I then established Youth Dimension (YD) with the express purpose of reaching young people in secondary schools and discipling young adults in their walk with Jesus. I retired in 2014.

I've experienced street evangelism, spoken at secondary-school gatherings where over four hundred students would sit enthralled by the gospel, worked with raw youth to see them rise to positions of influence in churches, and seen a season where every church wanted to work in secondary schools. I've had the privilege to preach in youth rallies, evening church services, Sunday School anniversaries, on beaches, in homes and in small Victorian rural churches and community centres. The stories and principles of ministry and life that have come out of my experiences have been so numerous, I felt I had to write about them. It's a bygone era, the time when this style of ministry worked so well. Yet I believe the lessons learned remain true and useful to this day.

Pam and I have three children who are married and have given us ten grandchildren. What a blessing! Currently one couple work in church pastoral Ministry and in an art shop ministry to locals, another has a church plant in Healesville, Victoria, and the other pair heads up Noosa Hillsong church. Each one has a bearing on our story.

I have written this book with the intention of helping the reader feel what I have felt, even though the context of our lives may be very different. Regardless of whether it is my own personal story or the adventures we have had in YD, it is through storytelling that I have sought to encourage and enrich folk in their walk with the Lord. I believe God does ordinary miracles with ordinary people like us.

This book contains moments, not a life story. It is not an in-depth memoir but a collection of snapshots. It is for the most part in chronological order, though the snapshots may jump a number of minutes or a number of years.

My reflections are deliberately short and sweet and don't go over every detail. Why? For two reasons. One, I can't remember my entire life's story – and if I could, it might get boring. Two, it's so you can read a chapter, grab a thought and suck on it yourself. This book is designed for the person who, like me, can easily read a few pages in bed at night, get tired and fall asleep with the book balanced on their nose! My problem is, when I next pick up the book, I have to reread pages and pages to get the storyline all over again. Here, you can just mark your place and pick it up where you left off.

My heart's desire is that as you read, you'll be encouraged in your own walk with Jesus. I hope you also find it fun. Suck on this!

Rob Coyle

**I will remember the deeds of the Lord; yes, I will
remember your miracles of long ago.**
Psalm 77:11 NIV

Memory Stains

Two little black and beady eyes stared down at me. The furry legs gripped tightly to the edge of the quilt and my heart stopped beating in absolute terror.

I had just dreamed a spider was on my bed. When I opened my eyes, there in real time was a daddy longlegs spider staring down at me, wishing me 'Good morning'. I was six and petrified.

Was this a scene from a film called *The Revenge of the Spiders* being played out in real life? As a child, I used to pour kerosene down trapdoor spider holes and throw a lit match into their tiny burrows. The spiders would come careering out looking for the fire brigade, and I would giggle in delight. Sydney was a great place for a six-year-old like me to face his fear of redbacks, funnel-webs, trapdoors and all kinds of creepy crawlies!

There are quite a few memory stains from my childhood that, like this one, can't be removed to this very day.

Is it true that the older you get, the clearer the memory of childhood moments? I don't know. Yet I can remember, as if it were yesterday, another occasion of lying on that lime green quilt on my single bed – the same bed and quilt I had met my daddy longlegs friend on – but this time, I was crying as my dad walked out of my bedroom. You always remember crying moments, particularly if you are a non-crier. Face down on the bed where the spider had sprung its peek-a-boo moment I cried, but not because of furry legs.

It's over sixty years ago and I still remember. It's a stain. Words alone had been exchanged between father and son, yet these caused my tears to soak that worn old quilt.

Some memories never fade. In fact, some memories can become even more focused as the years hurtle by.

What memories stain your present day? I'm about to tell you a story of miracle after miracle that have stained that six-year-old's life up to this present moment. One could argue that it all began on that bedspread.

A Dangerous 'No'

My mother was yelling words to the effect of, 'Will you get off that boy's back?'

Mum and Dad passed away many years ago, but I still I remember some of these times as though it were yesterday. How many words across a lifetime of parenting does a parent say to their child? A more interesting question: How many of those words does the child remember?

I can't recall the exact words Mum yelled at Dad that day, or even the words that made me cry, but I know why my lime green quilt with the red and green diagonal stripes was drenched with my tears. Simply put, Dad had asked me if I had Jesus in my heart and if I wanted to take that step of letting him into my life.

Six years old, and I had said 'No' in my heart to both questions.

I hadn't exactly shot the prime minister, stolen the Ashes or hijacked a jet plane. I was only six, for crying out loud! Mum was on my side. All I had said was "No" to Dad – and to Jesus.

Mum just didn't get the whole Christian thing. Dad had told Mum on their wedding night that he was a Christian, to which Mum had replied, 'So am I – I go to church!' Now the religion issue was back again, only this time it involved their only child (at this point in time). The issue of God loomed large in their relationship. I didn't realise, but I was the salami in this sandwich of a Christian marital dispute.

As time ticked by, the God issue got worse, not better. My parents fought quite publicly in front of me about a whole bag of issues. Once after a fearful argument, Mum put a hammer under her pillow and told me, her six-year-old son, that she would brain Dad when he was asleep!

But I digress. Which is the greater sin: embezzling a million dollars from your employer, or saying no to God?

While you suck on that one, here is my observation after a lifetime: it's a dangerous practice to say no to God.

There could be no miracles in this six-year-old's life till there was a 'Yes'.

Today, if you hear his voice, do not harden your hearts …
Hebrews 4:7 NIV

Crumbs in the Sheets

I can picture, even now, Mum putting that hammer under the pillow to fix Dad up during the night. Fortunately, it never happened. But I can remember Mum throwing a shoe at Dad. It missed him and went clean through a window, which luckily was open.

Do you know the result of having brekkie in bed? If you eat your toast like I do, crumbs go everywhere. No matter how much I try to brush them out, I'll still find some uncomfortable crumbs in my sheets when I get back in.

Some people have no memories of their folks fighting. I have a whole library. Wow, these guys were volatile. They were like two petrol tankers driving at maximum speed towards each other, and great was the explosion therewith. I can also remember some incredibly happy family moments. They were as sweet as an over-sugared pavlova.

Deep down inside, despite the dramas, I knew they loved each other, but there were crumbs in the sheets. It was not a comfortable relationship. Crumbs in relationships can really irritate. The crumbs in my parent's relationship caused them to separate, for months at a time, on at least two occasions in the early years of their marriage.

There were many crumbs in there that don't need to be put in black-and-white print. But there was one crumb in their relationship that, unless dealt with, would destroy them: religion.

Don't you hate crumbs? We have all got them, and they make sleeping at night uncomfortable. Sometimes the things that keep us awake at night need to be vacuumed out of our life.

At this point in time, it felt like Mum and Dad needed more than just a good vacuuming. They needed a miracle.

Do not be yoked together with unbelievers. For what do righteousness and wickedness have in common? Or what fellowship can light have with darkness?
2 Corinthians 6:14 NIV

A Loaf of Bread

He sat as a fourteen-year-old, transfixed. Eventually that night, he was transformed by what he heard from this Christian missionary doctor. Doctor Paul White was speaking in a home meeting in Sydney.

This was the moment when my Dad became a Christian.

A number of years later, as World War II raged on, Dad met Mum, whom he affectionately called 'Bubby', and they married. He had long slipped away from his relationship with Jesus. But ultimately, Dad was a Christian and Mum wasn't.

A non-Christian marrying a Christian is more than an irritating crumb between the sheets of married life. It's a full loaf of bread.

In over forty years of working with youth, I still see that same loaf of bread between married couples' sheets. I have people tell me of amazing conversion stories through 'missionary dating', where a Christian has led a non-Christian partner to Jesus. But for every one of those I hear, I could tell you ten more where that loaf of bread has destroyed the marriage. I have lived in such a family and, quite apart from the biblical injunction not to do it, my heart yells from experience, 'Don't!'

When I was around five, my dad came back to the Lord. He was sitting in a suburban park eating his lunch, minding his own business. From nowhere came a man with a sketch board, preaching Jesus to the sedate, lunch-eating crowd. The words the outdoor preacher shared were arrows of conviction to Dad's heart, and he turned his life around there and then.

Before that, Dad had stolen eighty-seven items belonging to people around our neighbourhood. He returned every single one, including the mower taken from the neighbour next door!

Even though she believed in God, Mum just didn't get Dad's radical life change. Mum's parents wanted to send Dad to a psychiatrist to unravel his sudden enthusiasm for 'religion'. They didn't get the Christian thing either. Dad's new love for Jesus helped split my Mum and Dad.

Mum left Dad twice. The first time, she simply disappeared to outback New South Wales. I was four and only remember being alone. Mum returned to Dad, though I don't know why – I was never told. The second time she left, it was with my auntie and us kids. Dad knew where we were. After six to nine months apart, we returned.

How much does a child know of what really goes on between their mum and dad?

I am amazed they stayed together in the light of all the pain it brought. It was a miracle they stuck it out. They made it until Mum came to the Lord when I was sixteen. Life changed. My abiding memory of Dad and Mum's later years is of them sitting up in bed each morning, cups of tea in hand, reading the Bible together. It was a miracle.

To me, Dad was my hero. But there were a few crumbs in our relationship, too – after all, I'd said no to my hero.

How many young people live chained with the feeling they have disappointed their parents? Their parents' expectations of great marks, significant careers, unbelievable sporting achievements and much more become a weight around their neck as big as Jupiter. It can bore into a kid's psyche like a termite, chewing through their self-worth.

Of course, the main problem was not that I'd said no to my hero. It was that I'd said no to Jesus. A reckoning day was coming, because six months later another voice was to challenge my child-like heart.

A Brown Van with Yellow Writing

I think life is the opposite of a colour photograph fading with time. I suspect that as we grow older, more colour touches our memories.

Well, here goes – I think this is an accurate retelling. I'm trusting there is not too much added colour!

I went to Barker College in Hornsby for eighteen months – that was as long as my parents could afford. In that private school, I topped the Prep class. I was given a prize for being dux among the four- and five-year-olds. I don't know what the other Preppie thought – 'cos there were only two of us! I ate my lunch in a cupboard for fear of the kids in the level above me. They were bullying me. It was not a happy eighteen months.

So, starting at Mount Colah State School, about thirty kilometres out of Sydney, was fun. It was a frisbee throw from our house, with around fifteen to twenty neighbourhood kids attending.

It was just another day at school. As far as I can remember, it was a brown van with yellow writing on the side panels. It pulled up under the monstrous ghost gums that were in our country schoolyard. Some unknown man pulled out a sketch board and talked to a curious bunch of kids about Jesus during our lunch-time break.

At the end of the program he handed out a prayer on a card. It had a place to write your name if you wanted to ask Jesus into your life. This time, there was no parental pressure. This time, I responded by signing that card. I wrote 'Yes' to Jesus … and then I hid it so Dad couldn't find it! To use old-time language, I was 'born again'. Anyone born again is the site of a miracle.

The unknown children's worker never saw me again. He was never to know I would become an evangelist in schools. Many, many times I have preached and sensed God moving, yet seen little outward response. It can leave your heart flattened like a tyre blowout. That unknown children's evangelist was not to know that a little seven-year-old came to Jesus that day, nor how the Lord of the Harvest was to use him to win hundreds to the kingdom. He may well have walked away deflated from his ministry in our school that day.

We are going to get some enormous surprises in heaven. God's word is alive, and I really believe his word does much unseen work we will never know about.

Was I ever to learn this lesson later on!

So is my word that goes out from my mouth: it will not return to me empty but will accomplish what I desire and achieve the purpose for which I sent it.

Isaiah 55:11 NIV

A Javelin

I had been to eleven primary schools but only attended one secondary school. My favourite subjects were lunch, morning and afternoon play and, best of all, holidays. Is there anyone out there who identifies?

I was a champ at arithmetic, but algebra, geometry, trigonometry ... I was lost. My brain just disappeared down the drain hole into a black nothingness.

Do you remember that engulfing feeling of sickness in your stomach at the thought of going into a certain class? That feeling of drowning in a whirlpool of non-comprehension as others seem to swim through it with Olympic ease?

I can remember trying to learn formulas. I just couldn't put them into practice. I felt like a brain surgeon trying to operate with a hammer and chisel. I was lost. I was too shy to ask for help. I just kept floundering without a yelp.

I remember sitting one day in my Year 9 maths class, on the right-hand side of the classroom towards the back, one of sixty students. I sat there and thought, 'I'm gone'. I knew I would never catch up. I can identify with those who feel that mind- and heart-stopping feeling: 'I'm dumb, and it ain't going to change.'

This all peaked in Year 9. It was the year I grew tall enough to move out of shorts to long pants, kind of like getting your blue pen license in Year 4! At the same time, I was being dumb in my walk with God. I was learning to swear. I was learning to tell dirty jokes to impress my few friends. My memory of Year 9 is a blur, but I know it wasn't my finest hour. To a non-Christian, my behaviour would not have looked shocking. I was just being a normal, obnoxious Year 9 boy. I wasn't all that bad. Yet I knew, deep down inside, I was kicking dust in the Lord's face.

Two significant events happened around this time.

The first is still so clear in my memory. The first event was in Room 8, a science room, where I was spinning another crass joke. I can't remember the joke. I can't remember the person. But I do remember one of my classmates saying when I was finished, 'Coyle, I thought you were a Christian!'

It was like a javelin flew through the air and pierced me, nailing me to the wall. I quivered, legs dangling, under its impact. I've never forgotten it, and I cringe inwardly when reflecting on that piercing conviction to this day. It shook my small, rebellious, confused heart. It prepared me for the larger javelin that was about to come.

Don't let anyone tell you God doesn't chase his sheep, because here was the Good Shepherd chasing me.

Did I want to be found?

What kind of javelin would he have to throw next?

> **Then he calls his friends and neighbours together and says,**
> **'Rejoice with me; I have found my lost sheep.'**
> Luke 15:6 NIV

A Collision of Two Worlds

At Ringwood Secondary School, the girls who stood for Jesus far outnumbered the boys.

Dad, from the day he found out I was a Christian, took it upon himself to keep me accountable. I hated it when he asked me, 'Did you go to ISCF today?'

Inter-School Christian Fellowship (ISCF) was one lunchtime a week. My recollection is that about fifteen students went, nearly all girls. I figured that if I sat in a certain position in Room 20, among these other Christians, then very few people could see me through the windows. I was afraid to be recognised as a Christian.

School was an excuse to play cricket and footy with the boys and hockey with the girls. It was not the place for 'church'. In my Year 9 worldview, church and Christianity were the same: church was the Sunday component of the week, and you don't play church or Christianity at school. Why the heck was my dad so hung up on me meeting with Christians at school?

So there I was in Year 9, doing my version of rebellion – but in disguise. I didn't want the church crowd to collide with my school life. I wore a disguise to cover the Christian life. (I figure I'm not the first to play this game.)

Can you see why the statement 'Coyle, I thought you were a Christian' nailed me to the wall? My two worlds collided! It happened with King David when confronted by Nathan the prophet. It happened with Ananias and

Saphira when confronted by Peter. And it happened to a confronted Rob.

The biggest javelin was yet to be launched. Though I'd been nailed to the science room wall by the statement that exposed me, a bigger revelation was coming. It was to hit me from behind when I least expected it. This was all leading to a miraculous change in my life.

The Lord is so unpredictable.

> **'For my thoughts are not your thoughts, neither are**
> **your ways my ways,' declares the Lord.**
> Isaiah 55:8 NIV

A Red AWA Radio (aka the Second Javelin)

What did the neighbours think? They'd be hanging out the washing or pulling the lawnmower out of the garden shed when they would hear a seven-year-old child's voice in a falsetto tone, giving the call of a jungle ape. As a kid, I often did this after listening to the serial Tarzan on the radio. (This is giving away my age!) Tarzan was my hero as a child. Who was your childhood hero?

As a teenager, my heroes changed. Apart from my dad, the majority of them were sporting heroes. If you are under forty, the names I revered would mean nothing to you. Heroes come, and heroes go. But the common denominator among them is that if you were in their presence, you would be gob-smacked, mute, stunned – reduced to a stammering, gibbering mess. Well, at least I would be.

I did what lots of teen boys do: I made up games where I played for, with or against my heroes. I had many years alone. My brother Paul didn't come onto the family scene until I was ten and my sister, Zayda, until I was sixteen. Because the age difference was so large, I lived like an only child. My imaginary heroes filled the void.

There was one hero, however, who was not only my hero but Dad's hero, too. This hero scared me, inspired me and left me mesmerised. He didn't play sport – he preached.

Unless you were around for the 1959 Crusades of Billy Graham in Australia, you just can't appreciate what an incredible impact Billy Graham had. His preaching was simple. His integrity was beyond belief. His presence came with an authority only God can give.

Can you imagine 100,000 people turning up to the MCG in Melbourne to hear a preacher today? Add to your imagination gazing at a tiny, talking pinpoint from the top deck of the 'G' – because that's how big Billy Graham looked to the crowds without the big screens we have today. Throw in a PA system of 1959 vintage, where the preaching echoes as if Billy was preaching in the Grand Canyon. That's what it was like. But people came regardless of the challenges of a large stadium, and they listened and responded. The whole event, particularly on the last day of the crusade, was amazing. God used this man.

I still remember the moment. We had a red-and-white AWA radio in our lounge room. I don't know why I was home by myself or why I put the radio on, although now I realise this was a divine appointment. I remember the words of this evangelist coming in short bursts, like machine-gun fire. In that lounge room, in the dark, I was alone with God, and my whole life did a U-turn from that moment on. God spoke to me like I'd never experienced before. Can I remember what he said? No – but God spoke to me. A miracle had happened. When the Lord speaks to you, life is never the same.

I have preached and seen kids the same age as I was, fifteen years old, make decisions for Jesus, then tragically fall away. I have seen young people respond in emotion and then go as flat as Coke in an opened bottle. This moment for me went beyond that. It was a moment where everything changed for me, forever.

Why do I describe this moment like a huge javelin in my heart? It was not just the moment but the incredible impact it had on my life in the following years. Jesus was to change me miraculously.

Billy Graham will never know this side of heaven of the way the Lord used him to impact a nobody – this Year 9 Aussie boy. The word of God, sown into the soil of human hearts, can spring forth into an abundant harvest. Heaven will reveal those who have taken in the seed.

So neither the one who plants nor the one who waters is anything, but only God, who makes things grow.
1 Corinthians 3:7 NIV

My Greatest Blessing

Do you like having your photo taken? Are you like me in that, when you see a family snapshot, your first impulse is to check yourself out? Ah, how the birth of the 'selfie' has increased our photographic addiction!

As a teenager I didn't like having my photo taken. The reason: when I was around seven years old, I had one of my front teeth snapped off diagonally and the other front tooth cracked. A wayward stick of wood smacked me across the mouth in a game of backyard hockey with my best mate. The cracked tooth went as dark as Cadbury's Old Jamaica chocolate.

What teenager likes that look? I looked like I had a tiny white iceberg and a burnt paddock for two front teeth! Added to that, I had so many freckles on my face, some school kids called me 'Fly Spots'. I didn't feel awfully happy about myself on the inside, either. It's true of many young people. If my value had been based on looks, I'd have gone for a fire sale price – or so I felt.

At secondary school, I remember Mr Harris, a woodwork teacher, giving me a mouthful about my appearance in class. His words were like acid on my already scratched self-esteem. I had come in from lunch, sweaty and red-faced, with socks down, all dirty knees and filthy shoes. He said, 'Look at you, Coyle ...' and, starting from my dishevelled hair, he moved gradually down my skinny frame, letting me know how horrible I looked all the way down to my shoes. I bet that you, too, can still remember any hurtful things said about your appearance. Doesn't it burn you deeply?

Girls scared me. My perception of my appearance made me worry that they would never be interested in a guy who had the appeal of the Hunchback of Notre Dame with chicken pox!

It's no secret that in your teens your hormones are playing havoc with your feelings on a grand scale. I probably felt no different that eighty percent of you reading this as you reflect on your teen years.

The tragedy for me, as with heaps of other young people, was that I had no one to share this pain with. Dad was my hero but not my close friend. I was like many other young men – I talked information with Dad, not feelings.

Talk to Mum? Mum had so much stuff going down at that time in her life, talk was impossible. Besides, as a teen, I believed that you just don't talk to your mum about personal pain.

Tell my friends? No way! It would give them ammunition to shoot me down.

I was brought up in an era when a boy, or man (I didn't know whether I was a boy or a man!) just didn't share. All I knew was, I wasn't meant to cry or share.

The result was an incredible aloneness and loneliness.

This was to be my greatest blessing!

Never will I leave; never will I forsake you.
Hebrews 13:5b NIV

A Tree Up the Back

For some reason, Banjo Patterson, the poet, captured my imagination. I loved his word pictures of Australian outdoor country life. The Man from Snowy River was electric reading for any young boy full of adventure. There were wild brumbies, whips cracking and stallions galloping down steep mountain ravines. Whoa – I loved it!

In my mid-teens I had felt like a wild young horse, going where I wanted, when I wanted. Since my encounter with Jesus through Billy Graham, I felt like the Lord was the man from Snowy River cracking a whip and pushing me in his direction.

Some time after the Lord had hurled those javelins of conviction at me, I decided to double the length of my times with God. It went from fifteen Dad-driven, compulsory minutes with the Lord to thirty voluntary, hungry minutes with Jesus. I loved it so much I doubled it again to an hour and then again to two hours. All this was when I was sixteen years old.

By the beginning of Year 11, I was rising round five o'clock to spend time with God. I look back and think, 'That's unusual'. Why did I do it?

I can see the Lord used his Spirit to convict me of my sin and draw me closer to himself. But there was another factor – the accompanying loneliness of life drove me to find a friend. I was desperate for a friend to share with, and that friend became Jesus. Loneliness was the cracking whip that drove my heart to follow Jesus.

One day, I found Dad's prayer diary. He prayed for people on a regular basis, some monthly, some weekly and some daily. Right on the top of the daily list was my name, 'Robert'.

In 1957 we lived in a bungalow, twenty feet long and ten feet wide, in North Ringwood. I don't know why I remember that measurement in feet, but I do remember that Dad built it. There was a tree at the back of that bungalow. It was in the bush, about seventy-five metres from our back boundary-line fence. Around six o'clock each morning, Dad would go there to meet with God and pray. So at sixteen, early in the morning, I began to get up early with Dad and spend time with God. I don't know what he thought when I started to rise earlier, but he surely must have thought his prayers for his eldest son were being answered.

The deep throb of loneliness now came accompanied with the adrenalin rush of finding the Lord as a real person and friend. My loneliness had turned into my greatest blessing by driving me to Jesus.

My dad's prayers were answered. Never underestimate the prayer of a burdened parent.

Then Jesus told his disciples a parable to show them that they should always pray and not give up.
Luke 18:1 NIV

Another Tick on the List

Way back just after the ark landed, the Victorian Education Department implemented Education Week. During that week was a day when your parents could come up to school and see you at work. Of course, for the greater part, it was the mums who came, because the dads went to work and mums stayed home to be the housewife!

I was so proud of my mum. I knew she was a 'looker'. I knew people would look at her and go 'Wow!' She had the most gorgeous strawberry-blonde hair and a figure to match. I can remember telling Mum, 'Wear the mauve sack.' The sack, a straight short dress (well, short for those days) was the absolute bomb. I was so proud to own her as mum.

Mum was also on Dad's daily prayer list. She smoked forty cigarettes a day and was a binge drinker. (I knew very little of this drinking until much later in life.) Somehow or other, despite a few periods of long separation, Mum and Dad were still together. I didn't know it at the time, but in my primary-school years, Dad had actually threatened Mum. The threat was that he would take her only child at that time, me, away from her if she didn't come back to him. She came back.

Mum never went to church unless it was for something special involving her kids. Dad used to drop me off at the Ringwood Brethren for church on Sunday at 11 am, 3 pm (Sunday School) and 7 pm. After dropping me off there, he travelled on to Ringwood Methodist for their services. Why? He thought the 'Methos' needed to hear the gospel and that the 'Brethos' could look after his son's spiritual welfare. Mum stayed at home with my brother Paul until he was old enough to go to church.

With my life starting to fire up for Jesus, I decided at sixteen that I was going to get baptised. Mum came to church that night. We had no idea until months later, but this was the night that Mum came to the Lord. It was another tick on Dad's prayer list, another miracle.

> **Elijah climbed to the top of Carmel, bent down to the ground and put his face between his knees.**
>
> 1 Kings 18:42 NIV

Sold

A short, nervous Year 7 student stands outside a bustling Ringwood Railway Station. You can almost see the sweat breaking out on his forehead as another evening peak-hour train pulls into the station. It drops weary workers off on their long trip home. He takes a deep breath and stretches out his hand with some kind of leaflet. The fear of rejection beats down the door of his heart. Will the stranger take it or brush it away?

Do you know what a 'tract' is? It is a small leaflet about the size of a cigarette packet. Tracts normally spell out, very simply, how to become a Christian. They often start with a conversion story or a story illustrating a gospel principle, then they lead to a call for commitment.

Dad used to take me up to the Ringwood railway station to hand out tracts. Along with some other guys, he used to preach from the back of a carboot through a microphone as people poured out of the station to go home.

I look back and think, how did I give out tracts as a twelve- or thirteen-year-old? When the Lord got hold of me in Years 11 and 12 and through into teachers college, I voluntarily went up to the Ringwood station of a Friday night and preached just like Dad. It was the beginning of the Lord stirring my heart to reach people with the gospel.

There was a time when this method of street preaching worked, but we were way past that time. Having the right method at the right time was something I had to learn ...

Picture this: It's the mid-1960s and it's a balmy evening in the Victorian holiday town of Cowes. As the sun sets over the beach, a lazy seagull disappears beyond the caravans. Dads, mums and kids with blankets and chairs start to wend their way down to the beach. They stretch out on the sand with blankets covering their legs and stare up at a crudely erected screen on the foreshore. They are ready for the outdoor movies. My eyes bulge and my heart races when I see four- to five-hundred people sitting on the beach at Cowes ready to take in a Walt Disney cartoon – and a Christian film.

This was the kind of outreach a group called OAC did. In between the cartoon and the Christian feature film, there was a twenty-minute gospel message using a sketch board. What pressed my buttons was that the audience actually listened!

This trumped Ringwood Railway Station. This smashed our church's Sunday evening gospel meeting, where the only thing non-Christian was the paint on the walls. I was hooked.

You see, around the time I was eighteen, someone very significant walked into my life. Dad had been doing street evangelism with a group called OAC. The Victorian branch didn't do street preaching over the Christmas–January holiday period. They went to caravan parks and beaches along the Victorian coast and ran children's programs in the outdoors. In the evenings, OAC showed Christian movies and shared the good news.

Bryan Greenwood ran the Victorian branch of the OAC. At the age of eighteen, Dad introduced me to this larger-than-life character. He had this warm, engaging smile that said, 'I believe in you.' He took me under his wing, and before I knew it, I was spending five weeks away over January, doing missions in caravan parks and beach resorts. By now I was training to be a teacher. I had the time and the enthusiasm. I loved it. Bryan was the right man at the right time for the shaping of ministry and character within me.

I was so hooked, the second year around I was up to my armpits in the preparation for summer OAC outreach. Little did I know that this was to be a God-defining moment in my life.

Another Reaps

It was a chilly January evening. The fishing trawlers hauled up on the sand nearby seemed to tower over us like silent centurions guarding the nearby caravan park.

The first time I preached outdoors with OAC was at Newhaven, in a caravan park that used to sit on the right-hand side of the bridge that connected Phillip Island to mainland Victoria. I had learned how to use the sketch board. The board was a piece of ply around one square metre, propped on tripod pipe legs and covered with butcher's paper. I loved cartoon drawings and used them to effect as I preached. The problem for anyone using this method was not the drawing itself but drawing and talking at the same time. It was a skill that needed practice. You also needed the ability to disguise your artwork's final picture, so that the last sentence of your gospel presentation coincided with the last stoke of your paintbrush, revealing all.

There were about sixty holiday-makers in Newhaven on this, my first attempt to draw and share the gospel. I was like a Labrador pup with the butcher's bone. I preached my heart out.

Bryan, the Victorian Director of OAC, later told me that I sent them to hell and back quite a few times in my twenty-minute talk!

Got the picture? I was raw and ready, very shy yet desperate to preach. I owe much to Bryan's gracious and encouraging feedback. For over fifteen more years, I went with OAC over the Christmas holiday period, helping on (and eventually leading) teams running children's and adults' programs. I had to face many unknown, sometimes hostile, environments. It was to put steel in my heart.

Hundreds and hundreds came to our programs, which were incredibly successful at getting people to listen to the gospel. Newer delivery methods of entertainment like the internet had not arrived. Portable TVs were for the rich, and they weren't to be found in caravan parks. People had no entertainment. In terms of response, we saw many children come to Jesus, but very few adults.

I had no idea, absolutely none, that the Lord was teaching me a lesson I would carry for the rest of my life. 'One sows and another reaps' (John 4:37 NIV). I was to be the one who sows. I had to learn that a sowing ministry is legitimate.

The Flying Bus

At twenty-three, I had a small, old, pale blue Comer bus. I would pack twelve to fifteen kids in it, with no safety belts, and take it flying down a particularly steep dirt road. Near the bottom, this road flattened out for about ten metres, then dropped away again. If I floored the old bus, it would take off after the ten-metre flat spot. It had a big-dipper effect on the tummy, and the kids would scream with delight. Crazy, crazy, crazy, what was I doing!

So it was a strange thing to find myself kneeling down on that road, age twenty-five, about the spot where the bus would usually take off in flight. It was around 3 am on a crystal-clear night, with a moon shining its bright light down on the track. The bush crickets were talking to the stars and a normally unemotional Rob was emotionally telling the Lord, 'I'll do anything you want. I'll go wherever you want.' It was a line-in-the-sand moment.

I walked and prayed with God at this hour because I'd missed talking to him for a little period of time. Somehow, it had led to this moment on Glenvale Road, Donvale, where I once again surrendered my life. However, there was more to it than surrender – it revealed a heart desperate to know what God wanted. What did God want me to do? Surely, you've had such a moment. So moved was I, I had rashly said to the Lord, 'I'll go anywhere you want.'

Ever had the Lord test out your promise?

I went home, climbed into bed and thought I would read my Bible before going to sleep. It was a cosy, comfortable spiritual moment. I was feeling pretty dedicated. And then … I opened my Bible and to read this verse: 'Go rather to the lost sheep of Israel' (Matt 10:6 NIV).

I was stunned. I was paralysed. It was like God was saying, 'Okay, Rob. Anywhere, you say? Go to Israel.'

Now, I know the idea of guidance and how God guides is a prickly topic. I know one verse is dangerous without something a bit more substantial. Yet all I can say is, it felt like God was talking to me.

I did what most people do when confronted by God on something unpleasant. I explained it away. I said, 'That's not the Lord, it's my imagination.' After all, Russia is not in the Bible. Neither is Hawaii! Besides, Israel is all through the Bible. It was ridiculous to think the Lord would be telling me to go to Israel. Incidentally, all hell was breaking out in the Middle East at that time, so this direction was beyond palatable. There was no way I was going to get blown up by some Arab soldier. The idea scared me.

So I dismissed it. Instead of sleeping like the spiritual giant I had imagined myself to be because of my road-kneeling moment, I slept uneasily, hoping I'd wake up and it would all go away.

Isn't sleep a great escape mechanism? Jonah will tell you that! What would the morning bring?

But Jonah ran away from the Lord.
Jonah 1:3a NIV

Hit by the Ghan

How many times have you said 'Yes', and later thought, 'What was I thinking?' Here is such a moment.

I had completed a certificate in primary teaching and went on to do a certificate in teaching the deaf. After three years teaching the deaf, I headed off to MBI. (Melbourne Bible Institute)

I had entered Bible college, bravely saying in my heart, 'I will not be distracted by girls!' Now that's interesting, considering that so far in my life I had taken one girl out, once, and I was currently twenty-four years old and alone. The ladies weren't exactly falling over themselves for me.

I have met many young people since who make silly promises like I did to God. I don't listen to the foolish words but listen past them to hear how their heart is beating for God. Normally such craziness indicates a heartbeat that's very strong.

Do you know of *The Ghan*? It's a train that crosses the barren wilderness of Central Australia. It's big and long. If *The Ghan* had literally hit me at full tilt, I couldn't have been hit harder than what the Lord said one morning as I knelt by my bed at Bible college. There were six of us in a room. The bedroom was part of the Bible college dormitory. We all were dutifully spending time with the Lord from 6:30 am to 7:20 am in the morning. It was part of the college's schedule. The moment came when, kneeling beside my bed, the other five in the room faded and I felt alone with Jesus.

It was like the Lord picked up a megaphone and yelled one centimetre from my ear, 'You are flirting. You are leading this girl on. It's wrong!'

The Lord had given me and those who led with me, an incredible season of fruitfulness in a youth group we had led at Ringwood Gospel Chapel. It was life changing and heart shaping for me. Time had moved on, and now I was at Bible college and had left the youth group in the hands of a capable leadership team.

There had been a girl who had helped me and prayed with me about our outreach and youth group activities. Her name was Pam, and she had moved to 'unattached' status.

Pam and I were talking lots. It was not just about youth group but life. The talking was more frequent. There were no mobiles. There was one public phone available to the one hundred male students in the college. I would ring and talk to Pam about youth group. This wasn't easy, as I competed with the other ninety-nine guys in college for the phone. Yet, when I finally had the phone, I simply loved talking to her!

As I knelt by my bed, the Lord's arrow of conviction struck my heart. I liked talking without commitment. God's megaphone was now bellowing in my ear. This talking was flirting. I was doing it. I was using this girl to make me feel good, to feel good about myself. It was selfish. It was sinful, but I didn't want to get more deeply involved because it could hurt me!

Under conviction of sin, I prayed something along these lines: 'If this lady is for me, Lord, tell me.' There was a 'titchy' bit of smugness in the tone of my heart. I thought, the Lord won't tell me for three or so years, so there's no need for worry about commitment. I thought it would be one of those 'pray for it for months' deals I had with the Lord.

I opened my Bible to have my reading after praying. It was in Genesis. Now, there's a safe book. There are no Pams in Genesis.

About the third verse in, I read Pharaoh speaking to Abraham. 'Behold thy wife, take her, and go thy way.' (Genesis 12:19c KJV)

I was stunned. I don't think I moved for five minutes! How would you have interpreted this?

For me, *The Ghan* had hit. I consider this the start of a miracle in clear guidance.

Do It

We've all had those moments when we've thought, 'I can't believe this is happening to me!' How about those moments when everything seems to fade into static because some jaw-dropping news has just landed on the desk of your heart? It's like the world goes into slow motion and the people you see every day have a 'fuzzy' edge around them.

I stared and stared at that verse. It paralysed me. 'Behold thy wife, take her, and go thy way.'

I wanted to run. I'd said to the Lord, 'No distraction by girls.' Marry her? We hadn't even gone out! I didn't know important information, like … um … like …. what's her middle name? I was frozen in fear.

This couldn't be right.

'No,' I decided. 'I have read too much into this verse.'

I can't believe what I did next. If you tell Pam, I'll have to drown you.

I ran tests. Was she like the girls I dreamed of – tall, blonde and so on? No. She didn't look like the girl I dreamed I would end up with. What guy hasn't asked himself the question, 'Is this the girl of my dreams?' This tells you more about men than it does about the women they're dreaming of!

However, she passed every question on spirituality I could muster. Except for one. 'Ah ha,' I thought. 'I've found a loophole.' Was she prepared to go into ministry, or even be a missionary? I was thinking of my Israel experience. By now, at least in theory, I had given in to the Lord and was prepared to go to Israel. Would she go to Israel with me?

I can't believe I did this, but I decided to put Pam to the test. In 1969,

Billy Graham was in town. Ralph Bell, an associate evangelist, was holding a youth meeting on the topic of 'Mission'. I could guarantee Ralph Bell would make a challenge to the audience and call out to the front of the rally any young people who would be willing to go anywhere in mission. I took the whole youth group in, with Pam, with the sole purpose of seeing if Pam would respond.

My fear of commitment reached its heights when Pam shuffled quietly by me in my seat and went out the front. On the way home in the car, she said, 'I don't know why I went out.' I knew! I was stunned.

This incident weighed on me heavily, like an elephant sitting on my heart. The Lord was telling me to go to Pam and start the relationship. I had given Jesus three months of excuses about why I couldn't start a relationship with Pam. It had to end. I had to face the terror of the uncertain waters of relationship. I couldn't run away anymore.

But how do people start a relationship? I had no idea. No one had told me. I had never understood girls. They were as mysterious to me as a John Grisham novel with no ending.

The Lord just kept on nagging me. 'Do it! Do it! Do it!' I was ready to give in, but how? Would she reject me? This is possibly every guy's nightmare. It certainly was mine.

An Awkward Moment

I can take you to the spot. It's where you drive into Eastland, a shopping centre in Ringwood, on Warrandyte Road. Forty-five years ago, or near enough to that, that was *the* spot. There was no Eastland then.

After church (don't all big events happen after church?) I stood on the footpath mumbling to Pam that I wanted her to pray about us getting together and to let me know what the Lord told her. It was hardly spectacular. In fact, I'd barely stammered it out when an old friend pulled up in his car and I wished Pam goodbye. I just left her standing there. I felt as awkward as a pelican born with a budgerigar's beak.

I rang her on the following Wednesday from college. Pam said, 'I've got an answer', then kept talking about other stuff. I was none the wiser to the answer. How often can you kick yourself for being dumb? I had boot prints all over me. Why didn't I ask her what the answer was? I'll tell you. I was numb about the thought of having a girlfriend from God.

The next day was Easter Thursday, and we were let out of college. Pam came to our place for tea. Mum and Dad must have known something was going on, but I never talked to them about personal matters. The rest of the family drove out after dinner to leave on an Easter holiday break. We were alone, washing the dinner dishes. I asked her what the answer was to her guidance about us. When she said 'Yes', I said something deep like 'Great!' There was an awkward silence, and we discussed how the Lord had led her to that point.

Once that was done and dusted, I remember thinking 'What do I do now?'

Over the fifty years since that dish-washing moment, I can reflect on how there has been so much to our journey. At that moment, we had no idea about the crises, sorrows or joys we were to face together. We only knew one thing at that point in time: God had put us together. That's all we really knew. We knew it from the start of our relationship, which is unusual, because most couples don't have that certainty till much later. The Lord was so gracious to us. It was miraculous guidance.

That one simple fact, 'God had put us together', would be a strong foundation during many an earthquake in our life's journey. It put concrete in our relationship.

I being in the way, the Lord led me ...
Genesis 24:27 (KJV)

Israel

While at Bible college, I would pick up this cute little brunette every Monday from outside the Lilydale Commonwealth Bank.

At MBI in those days, you had Monday afternoons and evenings off until 10 pm. If you weren't in by then, you were dead in the water.

My old boss, Bryan, gave me a super bit of advice about relationships: pray and read your Bible together. So every Monday, Pam and I would pray and read our Bible for around an hour. The practice of spending time together with the Lord, we were to discover, was harder when we were married. Have you found that? Yet before you are married, you think it is going to be easier.

One day in Pam's smoky, faded green Cortina, out in the empty blocks of land on an estate called Chirnside Park, we were having a quiet time with the Lord. We sat there stunned. It was just one of those moments. I can't even remember the verses, but they gobsmacked us. We had read words along the lines of, 'You wicked and rebellious children.' Pam had flatly refused the Lord's call to go to Bible college. I had been running from my Israel experience. I was ignoring God's call in the secret compartment of my will.

Do you remember the verses I had read about Israel? Those verses I had read after my 'meet' with God on Glenvale Road in the middle of the night? By now I knew, via other experiences happening in my life, that the Lord was saying, 'Go to Israel.' Pam was sitting there thinking the Lord was saying, 'Go to Bible college.' We turned to each other with hearts pounding and shared what we thought the Lord was saying. We were both being disobedient.

Pam applied for Bible college. I applied for more information about being a missionary in Israel.

In 1970, Pam rocked into college. We waited and waited for the mission in Israel to respond to our enquiry.

Pam did not find college a pleasurable experience. (Maybe that's a topic for another book, entitled, 'Obedience doesn't always equal pleasure.') As far as I can recollect, it took in excess of six months to hear from our Israel mission. By the time the reply came, we were pumped and raring to go.

The letter from the mission came on a Monday afternoon. It was short. It was bordering on dismissive. It was a 'No'. We were confused. We had been obedient. What was going on?

That Monday afternoon, we read the Bible together and read this verse.

'What he opens no one can shut, and what he shuts no one can open' (Rev 3:7c NIV).

God had shut the door. Subsequent events verified the locked door. Was the Lord testing our obedience? Why? I'll never know this side of heaven. Unanswered questions can kill you. All I knew was, the door was jammed shut. I reckon many of you reading this will have unanswered questions, too.

What did the Lord want us to do? Our focus had been Israel. What now?

**See, I am sending an angel ahead of you to guard you along the way
and to bring you to the place I have prepared.**
Exodus 23:30 NIV

Miss Adams

'Miss Adams', Pam's maiden name, was how I was supposed to address her at college. It sounds funny, calling your fiancée by her surname. Melbourne Bible Institute, now called Melbourne School of Theology, is rich in heritage. There are many stories of great saints sent to the four corners of the globe from this institution. Miss Adams (my Pammy) was addressed that way because MBI taught respect for the opposite sex, so to call her Pam would have been too familiar – and that was not on.

Except that the year Pam came, they changed the rules!

I had been there a year already under the old regime. In that year I had been elected, along with ten others, as a kind of prefect to help govern the student body.

The rule change declared that you could now engage in natural conversation with the opposite sex and call them by their Christian name. By today's standards, I know this sounds ridiculous, but to the student body of the time, it was radical. It's peculiar how you can be shaped by your environment. I found it very difficult to talk to girls naturally and call them by their Christian name. Why? Because I was now a leader, and one who was convinced the old rules were okay. To embrace the new rule too quickly, I thought, would show me up as a person who didn't respect the old culture of college – and perhaps a bit of a flirt.

Now I will leave it to your imagination what pressures that put on my relationship with Pam at college. Here's a glimpse. I didn't go out of my way to talk to her, as I thought it would be a bad example to the student body. I struggled to call her Pam. I felt everyone was watching us and I behaved accordingly. Don't you hate it when you live to please people! It was complete 'Miseryville' for Pam.

Near the end of Pam's second year at college and my third, something unusual happened. We were praying about our future. Israel as an opportunity was now buried.

I was walking across the lawn to the men's common room with the OAC prayer letter in my hand. I hadn't bothered to read it; it was just another prayer letter that came in the mail along with many others I received. OAC, by now, had been part of my life for around eight years, and I was used to their letters. I saw Pam and yelled out to her and gave her the prayer letter to read. It was printed on a piece of mauve A4 paper.

About three minutes later, Pam told one of the guys to grab me from the men's common room. I came out a little agitated. Pam simply said, 'Read this', and handed me back the prayer letter.

So I read the first paragraph – blah, blah, blah – and then there was a verse, followed by another paragraph of blah, blah, blah.

I stood on the lawn transfixed. I could barely move. You know that surreal feeling you get in your veins when something momentous happens? For me, it's a combination of my body feeling numb, my head spinning, my mind losing traction on reason and a voice in the distance saying, 'This can't be happening.'

Pam just stood there with me.

An Open Door

It's August 1970. The OAC prayer letter, a regular monthly circular, is in my quivering hand. I'm standing on the Bible college lawn stuck to the ground by emotional superglue.

In 1969, Pam and I believed we were called to Israel, only to get a note from the mission we had applied to, from a Doctor Dwight Barker, which read:

> I am not sure I can offer you too much encouragement concerning the opportunities for Christian Service among the Jewish people in Israel ... one can usually come as a tourist for three months and usually have that extended for three months, then that is about the end of it.

And then there was the verse the Lord had given us the day after receiving the letter:

> What he opens no-one can shut, and what he shuts no one can open

(Rev 3:7 NIV).

We had felt the door slam shut in our faces, our noses ricocheting off the door handle.

But this! There I stood with Pam, mesmerised, on the college lawn. There, slap bang in the middle of the OAC prayer letter, was the verse that came directly after the one the Lord had used to stop us going to Israel.

I know thy works, behold, I have set before thee an open door, and no man can shut it (Rev 3:8 KJV).

I had previously been offered a staff position at OAC, but my sense of call was as distant as a lost echo in the Grand Canyon. Pam and I hadn't heard God's voice clearly on this matter or on our future.

But now, without a word spoken, we knew the door at OAC had been opened by the Lord and we were to walk through it. This verse gave us the ears to hear. Lots of other things happened to confirm our call, but this was the first green light to go – and go we did!

Reflecting on this since, I believe Pam was called first by reading the letter first. What's more, Pam was called equally with me, though she never took part in ministry events. My observation of people lasting in ministry is they only last as long as their partner's sense of call. If that fades, then it's all downhill from there. Solomon says, 'If either of them falls down, one can help the other up' (Eccl 4:10 a NIV). If your husband or wife is not with you, sooner or later you will find it too hard to be alone in ministry. A marriage or a ministry is just too much for one partner to carry.

If I am talking to a couple considering ministry, I tell them, 'Make sure you are both called.'

Here was one of the few incredibly clear moments the Lord shouted at us. It was a miracle.

The one who calls you is faithful, and he will do it.

1 Thessalonians 5:24 NIV

Preached Out

I have just finished looking through my 1972 diary, my first year in OAC ministry. It went at a pace that makes lightning look like slow motion.

Here's where I went in that first twelve months. See if you can work out how many of the places I visited are up country and how many are metropolitan. If you are not from Victoria, Australia, you won't have a sniff of a chance!

Port Melbourne, Yallourn, Nunawading, Warrnambool, Halls Gap, Grovedale, Boort, Barraport, Clear Lake, Box Hill, Ringwood, Belgrave, Geelong, Yarra Junction, Abbotsford, Warragul, Nyah, Piangil, Nyah West, Stawell, Hepburn Springs, Tooleybuc, Swan Hill, Keon Park, Dingley, Lorquon, North Melbourne, Carey Grammar, Pascoe Vale, South Warrandyte, Sydney.

This is a list of the places I preached at in my first year of ministry with OAC. Some of them were one-off programs, others were one-week missions – in some cases, they were two weeks.

For those of you wondering, over half are country locations. I preached everywhere. I preached a sermon on Samson twenty-one times. I worked out I was in over eight hundred meetings and I preached around five hundred times. I look back and think, 'Insane!' Yet, the experience I gained was outstanding.

A couple of things happened.

Firstly, in my first six months of ministry I preached my heart out and saw very little outward response to the gospel. It gutted me.

Secondly, it had an impact on my marriage. Pam and I were married in December 1970 and spent the first twelve months of our marriage in a shoebox of a flat on the MBI campus. Then it was headfirst into this year of crazy, frantic ministry.

We both experienced stomach-wrenching loneliness. I can't begin to explain how hard it was. When apart we would write letters to each other every day and desperately wait on hearing the postman arrive.

For Pam during these years, it meant bringing up toddlers for up to a third of a year with an absent husband. We were in OAC just under seven years. Our first daughter Kim arrived in 1974, followed by our son Jamie in 1976. Nicole our YD baby, came later, in 1979.

For me, ministry loneliness only increased as the family grew.

I look back, particularly, on our first year, and realise that it was strangely beneficial. Yes, I was preached out, but it challenged me to ask the hard questions. What were my priorities? Was I preaching for success? How should I handle so much time away when I had no control over my timetable? The questions went on.

I always knew that sacrifice would be part of ministry, but what should it look like?

An Iceberg Down My Spine

I was in a small bungalow at the back of a house, in Mitcham, a suburb of Melbourne. Not that I was conscious of either the bungalow or suburb!

I had come around to help counsel a guy in his twenties who had responded at a church service I'd spoken at.

We had been talking for a while. During this time, a gradual sense of being uncomfortable had moved to the feeling, 'Something is not right here.' A darkness enveloped me. A feeling that something was very wrong washed over me. This was followed by a deep dread of evil I couldn't explain.

No, this young man didn't threaten me – but in my spirit the alarm bells were ringing loudly. I was in danger. The body language, the words, the looks ricocheted off the walls back at me, screaming death.

I felt trapped and frightened beyond belief. I felt like an iceberg of fear was gradually sliding down my spine and I didn't like where it was heading. I talked, trying to maintain a calm appearance and at the same time giving reasons why I needed to leave. I eventually got out and drove home, shaking. I had feared for my life.

Years later, I think this was more than just a moment of overreaction to an unusual situation.

I think it was more than just a moment of teaching, showing me to pick my places where to meet people to counsel.

I think it was a moment of divine rescue. The Spirit was warning me of imminent threat and danger. It's hard to explain those moments, except you know it's not your imagination but God speaking.

I think there are, and will continually be, unexpected moments of

Satanic attack on God's children.

Therefore put on the full armour of God, so that when the day of evil comes, you may be able to stand your ground, and after you have done everything, to stand.
Ephesians 6:13 NIV

Young People

In my OAC years, I developed the ability to draw cartoons on a sketch board using poster paints and brush. As I have said before, this was an incredible medium to grab the attention of young people and talk to them about Jesus. People were mesmerised as a picture gradually took shape before their eyes. As I painted, I preached. It broke down resistance to hearing the gospel.

I used this method at camps, youth rallies, church services and in schools.

In these early years of ministry, camps were by far the most successful ground for gospel reaping. It was not unusual, no matter how difficult we made the opportunity to respond outwardly, to see fifty to seventy percent of camp attendees respond.

However, it was in schools that I got most excited, even though the response was not huge. The number of students who came along was enormous by today's standards. Large groups of students, from fifty to four hundred and fifty, would crowd into a classroom or hall to hear the gospel. The students would be transfixed by what I was painting. They would desperately try to work out what it was. Even better, they would come back the next day to hear more.

In my OAC years, working with young people was more than a third of my ministry. It was during this time that a fire was lit within me for youth. This fire would never go out. I felt a strong pull towards the work in schools. It was more than an interest; it was a call, a divine spark planted in my heart. The more I did it, the brighter it burned. I loved it.

In my final years at OAC, I had an image come continually into my mind. It was of a metal funnel – the type you use to pour petrol into your car. In my vision, I could see a whole generation going through that funnel, which was labelled 'secondary school'. As they passed through, they were given a chance to hear the gospel.

That picture still burns in my heart.

… pray for us that the message of the Lord may spread rapidly.
2 Thessalonians 3:1b NIV

Ben-Hur

'Bigger than *Ben-Hur*' is such a Baby Boomer expression. Gen X, Y and Z would say 'Ben, who?' The epic motion picture based on Lew Wallace's novel, set in Roman times, was a huge hit in 1959.

When I reflect on parachurch ministries in the 70s and early 80s, they fall into the *Ben-Hur* category. The schools movement, driven by Scripture Union (which at the time was called ISCF) was widespread. If my memory serves me correctly, they had groups in over three hundred secondary schools. Youth for Christ rallies saw hundreds attend. And OAC was growing. I wrote in my diary in 1975, 'I did six hundred and sixteen programs last year; not as many as the previous year.' I can't believe there is a flavour of disappointment in that diary entry. Our teams were sharing the gospel everywhere. We conducted over a thousand programs a year, and we were seeing some great fruit.

In 1977, my final year at OAC, we began an outreach ministry called 'coffee shop'. We saw many young people pour into scout halls, church buildings, tents, literally anywhere we could find a place for them to gather over the Christmas holidays. The opportunities to talk about Jesus over raisin toast and coffee were endless.

There was always a prayer room for each team. Team members were rostered on every thirty minutes while the program was running to pray for what was currently going on in 'shop'. On one particular night in Port Fairy, we were told that a drunken group was coming down to tear our shop apart. The prayer room became a place of desperate prayer. Incredibly, the threatening louts marching down the street towards us just melted away. Great was the rejoicing!

On another occasion in Warrnambool, we had been praying for a guy to come to the Lord for the whole ten days of mission. Nothing happened. As we closed the doors on our last night and were cleaning up the hall, there was a knock on the door. Guess who was there? The guy who we had been praying for. He came in and talked and came to know Jesus.

When I left OAC, this ministry came with me. Over the fifteen years that followed, it grew to sixteen teams, each of which had around twenty-five people serving. We had teams in Western Australia, New South Wales, Tasmania, Queensland and all over Victoria. These were the *Ben-Hur* years.

Isn't it peculiar how you don't recognise seasons until they are over? At the time, I didn't perceive that the thousands the Lord was reaching in Victoria and Australia through parachurch work in Australia was something that might pass.

Likewise, I didn't recognise my time in OAC was exactly that – a season.

As early as 1974, barely three years into full-time ministry, what had started out as an itch to reach young people in schools was growing into an irresistible passion to see young people come to know Jesus. I had a growing desire to reach every secondary school in Victoria, and to repeat this every four years. In those days, a good number of students left secondary school after four years. I desperately wanted every student to have one chance to hear the gospel. OAC was to be the womb from which my life's key ministry, YD, would be born, and I had no idea. This was a season of 'pregnancy'.

In OAC we had teams of two staff go out and do outreach in Victorian country towns and in metropolitan Melbourne. At one stage there were six on staff. Six evangelists! In my observation, evangelists are independent, fiery personalities. We weren't all exactly that, but there was a touch of us all being cut from the same bolt of cloth. We drove many kilometres, slept in many different beds, preached in schools, lounge rooms, country halls and churches and ate hundreds of lovingly prepared country meals – and we loved it. Why? Because we all loved sharing the gospel.

It was here in this context that I was learning what a team should and should not look like.

I am forever grateful for what the Lord taught me in our 'Ben Hur' season at OAC.

Don't ever forget that, even now, you are living in a season.

There is a time for everything, and a season for every activity under the heavens.

Ecclesiastes 3:1 NIV

Early Clouds

When was the last time you stood still and gazed up at that sky that seems to recede in an endless sea of blue?

I think the best time for me is when I am on holidays at the beach, reading a book (I hate swimming and getting sandy grit in my clothes and between my toes). I pause, look up at the sky and see if I can find pictures in the clouds.

In 1976, I should have looked up at the sky a bit more. Unbeknownst to me, the clouds were gathering, and a storm was brewing.

In April that year, I put an entry in my journal saying I had talked to my boss about specialising in secondary-school work. I asked if I could do a six week module of outreach in secondary work as a precursor for taking a place of being a specialist schools worker in OAC. My boss and the board chairman of OAC had a conversation about the concept of a specialist schools worker. I had recorded my perception. My boss didn't seem happy about it.

At that time, OAC was considering purchasing a campsite at Yarra Junction, a little country town not far from the edge of Melbourne suburbia. This got my juices pumping. I dreamed of some kind of national discipleship centre.

Here I was, barely five years into ministry, and I already had two unquenchable fires in my chest. One was to reach teens in secondary schools, and the second was to see young people mature in faith and possibly go into ministry. As I look back, I can see that these were more than the wild imaginings of a dreamer. They were the start of a bigger 'God touch' to come.

I didn't recognise this. Thirty years later, I came to see thousands a week reached with the gospel and a brilliant facility for interns to be trained in. The Lord is truly remarkable. I would never have believed it. I just didn't see the early clouds building towards YD being formed. I didn't put together the unsettling of my relationship with my boss, the desire for schools outreach and the possible camp purchase as indicative of something good. A storm preceded it.

Sometimes it takes a storm for something new to be born.

Then the Lord spoke to Job out of the storm.
Job 40:6 NIV

The Sky Grows Darker

You know what it's like when a storm is on the way, how jet-black clouds in the sky create a certain atmosphere – an intense sense of foreboding. Well, the clouds were gathering in my life.

I will never forget the day Mum rang the office and said bluntly, 'Dad has leukaemia.' It was a death sentence in those days. My heart was pinned to the wall with a sabre through it. As I reflect on this time, I can see that I didn't know how to process this news. My way of coping was to be strong and busy. I am amazed at the lack of emotion expressed in my journal. I simply didn't know how to feel.

This was the first cloud. But there was a second dark cloud gathering.

You know the expression, 'an elephant in the room'? That's where everyone pretends there's nothing happening when everything is happening. I had been given permission by the OAC council to be released from normal outreach duties to concentrate on a six-week secondary-schools mission to the Dandenong area. I was pumped with excitement, yet I just knew in the pit of my stomach this was the elephant in the room.

My mentor, friend and boss was giving out a vibe that suggested he was uncomfortable with the whole concept. He didn't feel the organisation was ready for such a move. We never spoke about this at the time, but the elephant was there. He wasn't happy with the specialist schools worker concept that I was keen to fulfill.

Years later, having now been a boss and worked with many keen young evangelists, I can actually understand why he felt like this. At the time, I couldn't. The clouds were gathering.

Mum told me years later that my dying Dad, who was on the board of OAC, had said, 'Robert will leave OAC.' I never found out why he thought this. I'm guessing he saw my unsettled heart. Although he didn't live to see the day arrive when I actually did leave, he somehow knew it anyway.

I didn't give Dad the credit he deserved for his understanding of me. Dad never verbalised things much, but I knew he always believed in me. He knew the curve of my heart and understood where my passion lay. Parents know 'stuff' about their kids that their kids just don't realise.

In the midst of the gathering clouds, our son Jamie was born – a younger brother for our first daughter, Kim. I wonder how my precious wife Pam coped with a hubby who dreamed much yet delivered little at home at this stage of life. I was consumed and overcome with where our ministry's future lay. All I remember of Jamie's birth was the doctor nearly dropping Jamie when he was born. He was a slippery little customer.

Here was a mixture of dark foreboding clouds and brilliant rays of sunlight in our lives.

Storm clouds were gathering, but a small shaft of light still shone – a new son. It is so easy to ignore those shafts when the darkness is closing in. There is great wisdom in that old hymn, 'Count your blessings; name them one by one.'

> **You snatch me up and drive me before the wind;**
> **you toss me about in the storm.**
>
> Job 30:22 NIV

Pause for a Hero

Dad was dying. My brother Paul, with what must have been a broken heart, had been taking Dad to healing meetings. Dad wanted to be healed. He had a group of folks who would come and pray over him and tell him he would be healed. At this stage of his life Dad was charismatic in his theology, so it was not unusual for all this to happen.

I, on the other hand, had been sent as a twelve-year-old to a conservative Brethren Chapel in Ringwood. I had worked with OAC guys, who likewise were conservative. I think Dad had me tagged as conservative. These were the days when anything involving the supernatural gifts was seen as wildly charismatic. The gulf between conservative and charismatic Christians in those days was huge. You were either a supernatural gifts believer or a conservative who fought for the biblical truths. Conservatives considered charismatics to be emotional religious hippies, and charismatics considered conservatives to be closed books. There was no middle ground for believing in both the Bible and the authenticity of supernatural gifts. In Dad's thinking, I wasn't the type to get involved in going to these healing meetings. In reality, I was still working out what I was, conservative or charismatic. I think confusion reigned, as you will see as you read on.

At so many levels, Dad and I didn't connect. We loved each other awkwardly. Yet I sense we both had a deep admiration for each other that was unspoken.

I have a birthday card he sent me while we were on holidays as a family in November 1975. He wrote, 'I've had a lot of pain in my chest and back. Living on pain killers since you left.' It's unusual for Dad to talk of pain and to write and tell me. It was about as vulnerable as Dad would get. His upbringing was military tough.

By the following November, Dad was critically ill. I wrote in my diary, 'The question of healing has come up again.' By December 27, I wrote, 'Dad is very tired and appears in many ways to have given up the will to live.' On January 3, I wrote, 'Dad went to see a woman involved in healing with Margaret Court, but he didn't get to see her and was disappointed.'

It's hard to watch your hero die. It was hard to watch as a family. I remember Dad saying to me, three days before he died, 'Why are you sad? I am going to see Jesus.'

My brother Paul took over the running of Dad's printing firm from that point on. He had just finished a degree at university. It had nothing to do with printing. Dad had briefly trained him. He did an incredible job in those early days with a grieving mum, a sixteen-year-old sister and a brother who couldn't even spell 'printing'!

Dad passed away on February 7, 1977. I spoke at Dad's funeral. Among other things, I acknowledged that the Lord had a choice whether to take the disease from Dad or Dad from the disease. He chose the latter.

I didn't fully grasp, till years later, how much impact Dad's illness and death had on my sister, Zayda, who was still at school, trying to pass Years 11 and 12.

Mum was to pass away many years later in 2004, and I need to acknowledge my sister's incredible role in supporting Mum through many difficult years. Mum never 'got over' Dad's death.

One final word on my father. Before Dad became incapacitated by leukaemia, he preached the gospel everywhere, including Fiji. While in Fiji, Dad saw over a hundred come to Christ in a month. It's this fire that Dad modelled for me, so excuse me while I pause for my hero.

The Israelites grieved for Moses in the plains of Moab thirty days, until the time of weeping and mourning was over.

Deuteronomy 34:8 NIV

Before You Know It

It was a weird shape, but apparently a very creative piece of architecture. It was the chapel at Carey Baptist Grammar School in Hawthorn, Melbourne. As I recollect, its floor plan was like a funnel in layout.

I remember thinking before one lunchtime program, as I so often did, 'Will they come? How many will come? It's out of the way from the school student area. Will they bother to walk this far?' Sure enough, the students came; around a hundred to a hundred and fifty came each day. They sat there quietly while I shared the gospel.

One of my first ministry opportunities in my early years at OAC was here at Carey Grammar, where two brothers, Tim and Peter Costello, were in Year 11 and Year 12 respectively. These guys got me into the school, and there in the 'funnel', for a week of lunchtime programs, I had this great opportunity to share Jesus.

Around three years later, in 1976, I was one of the speakers at a Monash Evangelical Union camp. Among those involved were again these two young men, Tim and Peter Costello. They had become great friends of mine. In the same year a young guy named Bruce Saward – a keen guitarist and just as keen for the Lord – was helping me out. Meanwhile, at my local church I had built up a meaningful relationship with Eric Price. How? I used to go around to his place to print a prayer points sheet for our church's midweek prayer meeting. He was about ten years older than me, but we just gelled in relationship.

I had no idea at the time, but God was bringing these guys together to be founding board members of the organisation we were to call Youth Dimension.

My observation of God bringing something together is this: he is working before we even know it.

Before a word is on my tongue, you, LORD, know it completely.
Psalm 139:4 NIV

What Were You Thinking?

When the board of OAC allowed me the six-week mission, where I did nothing but try to reach youth in schools, I chose to do this outreach in Dandenong schools. If you know the Dandenong area, you might say, 'What were you thinking? Some of those schools were like war zones.'

Tim and Peter Costello were helpful carriers of my burden to reach young people in schools, helping this solitary evangelist reach these broken schools. So, I launched into the six-week specialised youth outreach in Dandenong. I had been praying like a mantis for this for six months.

Dandenong is recorded over and over again in my journal. We went to Dandenong High, Hallam High, Doveton High, Doveton Tech and Cleeland High. I was scared. Doveton Tech was 'the' tough school of the area. It was a ravenous lion; it chewed up students and spat out the bones!

The first school was Cleeland High, where a Christian teacher named Roger Van Langenberg was an incredible help. We had two hundred and sixty on the first Monday lunchtime meeting … and fourteen on the Tuesday. I must have been gutted after Tuesday, but on Wednesday I saw a hundred and thirty return and on Thursday a hundred students come along. On the Friday we saw five come to the Lord.

At the end of each week, I handed out flyers advertising a Christian sports film. This was to be shown in local churches nearby. On the Saturday nights, kids would gather for this climactic event. I can still visualise the first one – a hundred and fifty Dandenong kids came. I had advertised it during the week in the local school.

I still recall that feeling of utter helplessness as I looked out on the crowd and wondered how I was going to share the gospel by myself.

I fumbled out a bit of the gospel after the film and then the youth left. For whatever reason, I hadn't engaged the local church in this attempt at outreach. My efforts felt as effective as using a box of tissues to mop up a tsunami. I had yet to learn how to engage the local church. I had tried, but they didn't get where this Rob Coyle guy ('Who is he, anyway?') was coming from.

Oh, I cringe when I think of those five Saturday night film nights in church halls during this outreach. Saturday after Saturday of trying to fumble out the gospel to crowds of around a hundred and fifty young people who just wanted to get out of the church hall after the film. Each Saturday night I would feel, 'Ugh, this isn't working.'

You would think this wet blanket of an experience would put out any fire I had in my belly to reach kids in schools. But all it did was to stir a fire in my heart to reach out to more secondary-school kids.

Take notice of fires that won't go out in your life!

But if I say, 'I will not mention his word or speak anymore in his name,' his word is in my heart like a fire, a fire shut up in my bones. I am weary of holding it in; indeed, I cannot.
Jeremiah 20:9 NIV

Crossroads

Life contains many uncertain moments. Try these on for size: Should I go through the traffic lights on orange or not? How about, should I drink this milk when the 'use by' date is today? Or, will she say yes to a date? How do you handle moments of uncertainty?

At this time, I was struggling with uncertainty like a mammoth on a melting iceberg.

The six-week Dandenong outreach was over. Now came the 1977 November OAC Committee's Conference, where they discussed whether to release me to do six months exclusively in schools The reaction was tentative, and I felt like I was running that orange traffic light.

The committee gave an unenthusiastic yes. However, by mid-December of 1977, the Victorian Chairman of OAC, a delightful businessman called Harry McKeon, wanted to postpone my six months release, because 1978 was OAC Victoria's 30th anniversary year. It was felt my schools work would distract from the anniversary event. The uncertainty grew. Would I be allowed to do it or not?

Add to this brew of uncertainty, some of my fellow OAC staff were not positive about the concept.

The pinnacle of uncertainty was reached with Pam asking me, at the end of 1977, the question, 'Why haven't we got unity from the Lord, if he is in it?' Pam was simply asking the obvious: if God's in this six-month trial, why the opposition?

Ouch! I'd rather drink milk that had expired than handle this.

At this particular time, Tim Costello and I were training twenty-four young people for a coffee shop outreach. It was to be in Inverloch in December, and we labelled the shop Drift Inn. 'Coffee shop' is an overrated way to describe this outreach. Yes, we served coffee. It was instant coffee of the International Roast variety. We sat on cheap chairs or on the floor on rugs. There were card tables covered in butcher's paper with a cheap-as-chips candles in the centre. The lighting was as dim as a goldfish. There was a prayer room, where there was a roster for someone to pray every quarter or half hour. Lastly, there were teams that went out on the street to invite youth in. Sounds crude in presentation – but it worked.

Years later, I discovered at least six of those team members on our first coffee shop went into ministry. I didn't recognise the great quality in our first team. In the midst of my turmoil over the future, I couldn't see the significance this ministry was to have for the kingdom. What is significant to God can so easily slip under our radar. It's often time that reveals what the Lord sees as significant in our lives – yet we miss it while it's happening.

I returned from our Drift Inn coffee shop to talk to Pam again, at great length, about our future. As my journal notes, Pam 'expressed a little uncertainty about our part in the young people's goals' (secondary-schools work). This impacted me significantly. Pam and I have always had this deal. We won't move on any significant decision in our life until we both agree it's the Lord's will. I felt like I had run into the back of a semitrailer on my push bike! However, the uncertainty also caused me to consider life outside of OAC and the insecurity that beckoned.

Many years later, I consider the moments that YD staff have come to me and told me, many times with a faltering voice, the Lord wants them to move on. They have stood at their own personal crossroads.

Are you standing at one now? He is standing with you.

But the Lord stood at my side and gave me strength.

2 Timothy 4:17a NIV

24 February 1978

It was early February when the council of OAC decided to cancel the six-month trial of a specialist secondary-schools worker. They said they were not ready for such a move. I felt I was confronted with an inevitable choice: stay, or leave and start another organisation. This thought terrorised me.

I visualise a sandy gravel road with straw-coloured tussocks of grass along its edge, occasionally punctuated by majestic giant ghost gums. Next to the track, the paddocks are hemmed in by old wooden fences made of railway sleepers, faded grey with time. As I drive along, the dust kicks up from the back of my vehicle. From a distance, it looks like a white cloud, billowing up behind me. I draw near to an old white signpost with four arms pointing in four directions. It's like a scarecrow that has lost its clothes. The letters on its arms are worn beyond recognition. As I gaze off in four directions, I see a horizon with no clues as to where I am. Which way should I go?

I'm sure you have felt that feeling just like I did – that feeling of standing at the crossroads.

Some people have unforgettable dates etched into their minds. February 24, 1978 is mine.

On that day, Pam and I talked at length about our future. Kim, our oldest child, was heading to three years old. Jamie was not yet one.

After talking to Pam, I prayed from 2 to 5 am. I was scared. I was a rabbit in the spotlight, staring down the barrel of uncertainty! What is God saying? Is God calling us out of this ministry that has been such a blessing to us? Do we believe God is saying, 'Move to where your heart burns'? Is it time to put our money where our mouth is?

Bryan, my OAC boss, had given one wise word of advice: I should do what the Lord told me. We'd had awkward moments since the announcement of the cancelled trial. Yet Bryan wanted the best for me. He also said that the Lord had told him not to hinder me. I regard that as miraculous, because everything else gave the vibe that he wanted me to stay. I so appreciated that comment. Not long after this, the OAC board gave me an ultimatum: return to my original job description or leave.

Pam and I went back to our original call from Revelation 3: 'I have set before you an open door.' On February 24, I wrote in my diary, 'That door couldn't be OAC, that door the Lord has shut!' The dye was cast. We had to move. We had to start our own thing. The verse the Lord had used to call us into OAC was the same verse he used to call us to a new ministry to young people in schools.

It took another four months before I walked out the doors at OAC, on July 6, 1978.

I continue to have the utmost respect for OAC and Bryan Greenwood. But I now wish I had jumped on February 24, when the original clarity came. My hesitation came through fear and a false hope that things might change at OAC. I was afraid of trying something new, and it stirred doubt.

That verse from the Epistle of James is so true – if you doubt, you are like a wave tossed about by the wind.

I am amazed at how the Lord enabled me to hang on in the face of my own personal uncertainty. Considering my temperament, which was saturated in a fear of making decisions, the Lord just kept holding us. It had to be the Lord that gave birth to YD, not me. It was a miracle.

It teaches me also to listen to the burdens that the Lord places on your heart. My problem was – and remains – discerning which 'burdens' are self-manufactured and which are God-given. Sometimes it's hard to distinguish between them.

Pam, Kim, Jamie and I had chosen which fork in the road to take, but with no resources. Where was finance going to come from? What about an office and admin help? Would schools still welcome me when I was an unknown quantity? How could we do it?

However, I knew it was what we were meant to do – with or without resources.

There is no better place to be than in the centre of God's will, no matter how foggy it may be.

A Full Vacuum

The carpet was purple. Brilliant purple. Would you ever buy purple carpet for your house?

There was a double bed in the room; it was the bed my dad had died on.

This was the first YD office! Mum couldn't sleep in her bedroom since Dad had died, so it was the only place free for the first YD office. Working out of our own home was never an option. I knew I would be tempted and distracted by our little family.

The day I left OAC, I walked not into a vacuum but into ministry.

The weekend after leaving, I took a camp with Balwyn Baptist. During the following week, I ran a series of Bible studies with Ian Purse's youth group at Heathmont Gospel Chapel. I was also in preparations to run a week of lunchtime programs using the sketch board skills I had gained at OAC. It was to be held outdoors at Bayswater High School.

Tim Costello and I had started a Bible study, training and sharing night called Taskforce. We held it every Wednesday evening from 6.00 to 7.30 pm at the old Blackburn South Baptist church. This was born out of the coffee shop outreach we had run at Inverloch the previous Christmas. I loved it!

Taskforce was made up primarily of Monash Uni students. There was an incredible buzz and desire to learn among this very special group of young adults. Tim had that raw ability to draw these young guys in. Tim and I loved preparing the Bible studies, and this fast-growing group seemed hungry for more.

At the same time, my mind was occupied with the possibility of a discipleship training centre at Macclesfield. Would Daryl and Robyn Redford, who were in OAC, come across to work with me in schools? Would I get enough people along to the schools outreach camp I had planned? What would the makeup of the ministry board be? How does the ministry become a legally incorporated body? What should this new ministry be called? (We hadn't thought of 'Youth Dimension' at this stage). And what would we live on?

I had feelings of uncertainty in plague proportions. 'Don't touch me; I'll leak unanswered questions!' Isn't it hard to listen to God when there is so much mind static?

God is our refuge and strength, an ever-present help in trouble.

Psalm 46:1 NIV

Two Babies

Pam and I prayed about if and when to have our babies. Even before they were conceived, we wanted to have a deep sense of our kids as a gift from God.

I know it's not everyone's cup of tea. I can't believe I had the space in my head to be praying about having another baby with all that was going down. But we made time to pray, and the end result was 'the baby' of our family, Nicole, who joined us in 1979.

Around the same time we were praying about a baby – 14 July 1978, to be precise – Bruce Saward (at this time studying accountancy at university), Tim Costello (also now a university student, training in law), Eric Price (a primary-school teacher from my home church), John Duke (a doctor and a friend) and I met for our first board meeting.

This meeting was held around Bruce's mum's kitchen table. Talk about humble beginnings! I don't remember much of it. All I wrote in my diary was, 'Went well.' John Duke was to withdraw from the board a month or so later, but he remained vitally interested in the ministry.

We adopted the name 'Youth Dimension' on August 17, 1978. I wish I had recorded the other name options. We chose this name because it carried an implicit rather than explicit message. We could explain ourselves by saying there was a dimension in life young people were missing out on – the spiritual dimension, a relationship with the Lord.

We were up and away, but the question remained: how were we to be funded?

This was the first real test of this new baby called YD. Would it be stillborn? Did the Lord really have his hand on us? Could the Lord do the miraculous and provide for us when we had brought very little financial support across from OAC?

My observation is that a new ministry often faces a faith test. You only have to recall Jesus' forty days of fasting in the desert and the Satanic onslaught afterwards to realise that even Jesus faced this test as his ministry commenced.

Don't be surprised at opposition when you are planning to poke the devil in the eye by heeding a call to a new ministry.

'Do I bring to the moment of birth and not give delivery?' says the LORD.
'Do I close up the womb when I bring to delivery?' says your God.

Isaiah 66:9 NIV

Uncertainty to Certainty

Since the age of sixteen, I have always been an early riser. Yet even for me, getting up at 4 am every morning for a week to pray for four hours is mind boggling. I was desperate, not spiritual!

We had no money, and a baby was on the way to make us a family of five. Schools missions, which involved week-long lunchtime outreach meetings, were multiplying like rabbits, yet obviously yielded no financial benefit. Our Wednesday night Bible study, Taskforce, was growing, but who can ask university students for money when they are broke? I was also hoping for Daryl and Robin Redford, fellow OAC workers and friends, to come and join me in YD, but that hope was fading. I didn't have a buddy to go broke with. I was still dreaming of a camp set-up for outreach and discipleship training, but that dream had popped like a soapy bubble.

So not only were we short of cash, but some of my dreams and hopes were sinking. I had read a book on the life of George Mueller. As a result, I had become resolute in my opinion that, like Mueller, I was not to ask for finance. I should just pray.

It's not hard to see that a combination of fear and faith drove me out of bed at 4 am every morning that week.

We not only needed finance, we needed people. We needed direction. At the same time, I was desperate not to let go of the Lord.

By the end of the week, $450 had come in. After two weeks, it was $700. (Back then, this was a lot of money!)

On Friday October 6, 1978, I wrote in my diary, 'Finance continues to pour in. The committee (YD board) undoubtedly was encouraged by answer to prayer. It must confirm the touch of the Lord on the ministry.' Over the years that followed, the Lord was to grant supernatural provision again and again.

Our second season of our summer coffee shop outreach, Drift Inn, saw fifty-two enlist to help. It was enough for two teams. Tim Costello led one team, and I led the other. We saw over twenty come to trust the Lord! The Lord had his hand on us.

There was another benefit to the success of this ministry – it gave us people. Many from Drift Inn came to Taskforce in 1979. This gave us an invaluable pool of volunteers.

My wife and soulmate stood like a rock with me. At the end of the year, I wrote of Pam, 'She has loved and cared for me through every anxiety.' Here was the greatest provision for my life!

Six months later, I journalled, 'The reading of my diary has refreshed me once again to see the greatness of the Lord in the forming of YD. There is no doubt – it is God's will.' Six months is not a long time, but it was long enough to bring closure to our time with OAC and certainty to our call to YD.

I knew then, and still know, that I couldn't do it on my own. In 1978 I had started out the year full of confusion and uncertainty, but by December 31, I was sure of my call. I had learned a lesson in guidance. Uncertainty to certainty comes most frequently through a process rather than in a single, profound moment.

> **The path of the righteous is like the morning sun,**
> **shining ever brighter till the full light of day.**
> Proverbs 4:18 NIV

A Film and a Sketch Board

IPods, iPhones, iPads, even mobile phones were all totally foreign to a teenager in the early 80s. Bear in mind, even colour TV was only five years old in Australia at that time. Walk into a secondary school in 1978 and show a 30-minute surfing film featuring mega wipe-outs, and you had an instant audience. Today, you wouldn't attract an ant!

It was the bait, the hook. Again and again, I would start off a week of lunchtime programs with a Christian surfing film called *Sunseekers*. It went off in the 80s! It had heaps of surfing footage, with a couple of surfers at the end giving brief testimonies. The film cost me $600 for the rights to show it, which was a lot of money, but over the following decade it brought in hundreds of kids. That film was worth every cent.

I would jump up at the end of this movie and say, 'Tomorrow I'm going to talk about the question, "Is it possible to contact the dead?"' The next day I'd get around half to two-thirds of Monday's audience. Three hundred to the film meant a hundred and fifty or two hundred to hear my sketch board talk on séances. Kids just came. Normally the size of Tuesday's audience held till Friday. On the Thursday, I would say, 'Only come back if you want to know how to become a Christian.' Numbers would then drop, in most cases by two thirds, but the kids who came wanted to know.

These were great years. This is what I did, week in and week out, when YD commenced.

The sketch board skills I learned in OAC were unbelievably helpful. Just imagine a double room full of two or three hundred secondary-school students. Now swallow this: you have to hold their attention for thirty minutes. Attendance was totally voluntary. The students could walk in and out at will. Being able to sketch was a huge help, and with my teaching background and growing experience, I started working out what held or lost kids.

Can you imagine what it was like doing this by myself, week after week? Or what it was like at some of the rougher schools, where students just didn't want to be at school and would let you know through challenging behaviour? I'll tell you more later – but I lived!

When [Jesus] saw the crowds, he had compassion on them, because they were harassed and helpless, like sheep without a shepherd.
Matthew 9:36 NIV

'V' for Victory (or Vanquished)

It's one of those random verses you read and skip over, like a flat stone bouncing across the surface of a tranquil pond. 'The men of Ephraim, though armed with bows, turned back on the day of battle' (Ps 78:9 NIV).

There are times when ministry can be a battle and everything within you wants to run away, along with the Ephraimites (Israel).

I was undertaking a week of lunchtime mission at a Western suburbs high school, a good forty-five to fifty-five minutes' drive from my office in Ringwood. It was a tough school. I had been to a school in this area only once before. At that school, they used to padlock all the classroom doors at lunchtime to keep the students out. Normal practice in schools was to leave classrooms open over break times. During my lunchtime program, I had kids climbing in and out of classroom windows.

As I drove west, I wondered what this school was going to be like. The programs were to be held in a theatrette that could contain three to four hundred people. The seats were staggered upwards from the front of the classroom. I started as usual with our surfing movie on the Monday. Over three hundred were in the theatre. It felt more like the Roman Colosseum. The noise, the pandemonium, the 'let's stir this up' attitude was crawling all over me.

I turned the movie off after a few minutes and issued a warning that I would eject troublemakers. It made no difference. I was in a den of lions, and I was lunch. At first, I kicked them out by ones and twos as I turned the projector on and off. Then I moved to kicking them out by rows. By the time the movie was over, I had booted out around a hundred and fifty kids.

How do you think I felt driving back to the office that day? How do you think I felt driving over again the next day to give a sketch board talk? I wanted to turn back on the day of the battle!

I thought, 'Oh well, there won't be nearly as many to hear me talk.' Wrong. There were nearly as many as the day before. When I turned around to sketch on my board, kids exploded in talk. Once again, I started kicking them out, a row at a time.

A whole row would march out, waving their hands in a 'V' for victory sign. It was slightly off-putting, to say the least.

This happened from the Monday through to the Thursday. I said on the Thursday, 'Come back tomorrow if you want to know how to become a Christian.' About the thirty came back, and around ten of them came to the Lord.

Every day I drove over, my feelings were yelling, 'Don't go'. My experience was saying, 'Waste of time'. but the Lord was saying, 'Don't turn back in the heat of the battle.'

I don't know which was the most miraculous – the ten who came to the Lord or my unwilling persistence.

**The men of Ephraim, though armed with bows,
turned back on the day of battle.**

Psalm 78:9 NIV

What Goes through a Preacher's Mind

The Lord graciously gave me many opportunities to preach in the 80s. I preached everywhere and anywhere.

I would often be shaking like a lamb before a pack of wolves that were coming off a hunger strike. Preaching in places like Melbourne Town Hall before a thousand young people made my heart quiver with fear. I would often think, 'You can't do this ... but it's too late now, you are on!' Other times, it was not fear that glued me to the floor in reticence but the voice of the evil one, whispering my faults of the past week in my ear: 'How can *you* be worthy to do this?' You can never guess what is going through a preacher's mind before they stand to deliver.

Some of the most significant opportunities were through Youth for Christ, an organisation that, among other things, ran monthly rallies with over a thousand in attendance. Clive Stebbins was the director, and he dared to believe in my preaching. For this I will always be grateful.

Evening church services were common and well-attended in most churches in the 80s. Even better for me, these were the services youth went to. I was invited to bucket-loads of evangelical churches to preach the gospel. I was like a pig in a mud factory – I loved it. I was so blessed to be in this era when non-Christian youth were frequent visitors in these congregations.

We saw many come to Christ. At the same time, the name YD became more widely known. I never spoke about YD when I preached, however, the association just happened.

The Fridge

There are some dirty, dark alleyways and deserted shop arcades you'd never want to take your mother-in-law into.

Our first official YD office was up one of these. It was the last shopfront at the end of an arcade that housed around ten shops, five either side of a covered walk way. We had moved the first YD office from Mum's bedroom to this suspect arcade. To give you an idea of how sleazy the arcade was, every shop in the arcade was robbed except ours. The local criminals must have realised there's not much money in Christian work!

The YD office had a high ceiling, which meant loads of excess space to warm in the middle of winter. We had huge patterned curtains, with white, fawn, brown and red swirls, for our shopfront window. The floor was covered with second-hand green carpet tiles. Some of you will be old enough to remember the sales pitch for these. 'Spill a spot on your carpet and you can replace the tile.' In our case, we had too many dirty spots and not enough spare green carpet tiles. The floor underneath the tiles was cement. The tiles were thin.

The huge shopfront windows got as cold as a policeman's handshake in the winter. The wind howled up the walkway, and the part-time YD secretary and I huddled over little heaters at our desks, trying to get warm. Little wonder I went through secretaries like a box of tissues in the early days.

Having said that, the Lord blessed me with a whole stream of great secretaries. The first, Rhonda Jones, worked out of her home doing loads of typing for me. Rhonda was married to Peter, my uncle. I will be forever grateful for the hours of unpaid work she did for me. Peter and Rhonda's financial support also helped carry our fledgling community.

After Rhonda, Robyn Wigney, Julie Farmilo and Debbie Reid (their maiden names) each came to work in 'the fridge' in Ringwood arcade. Not only did these women do great admin work, but they helped keep me sane as I continued to work by myself.

After them came a long-term secretary who was a tremendous gift from the Lord.

In the early 80s, Pam and I were running a small group. It was simply a delight to run. We had a whole bunch of adults who thought they were Christians but weren't – well, as far as we could tell. Breezing into this group came Linda and Gert Schaefer. Linda had an amazing story of God's work in her life. Pam and Linda formed a close friendship, so much so that Pam insisted I take her on as our next receptionist. Take her on I did.

I will never forget her first day. I think she broke the *Guinness Book of Records* for the most slowly typed letter of all time. She could barely type! I thought, 'Oh my goodness, what has Pam done to me?'

That day – May 24, 1985 – was, of course, a gift from the Lord in disguise. Linda went on to work for twenty years in the office, becoming the voice of YD.

Linda walked with me through all kinds of thrills and spills. These were the days when the mail was our financial umbilical cord. People didn't give by card, it was via the mail. Linda was the one who opened the mail, experiencing miracles of provision again and again.

Linda became a very proficient typist, but her warmth and love for the Lord and her ability to handle difficult people were her greatest gifts. I learned that the voice you hear on the phone, the first face you see when you walk into reception, sets the tone of an organisation. It required just the right kind of person, and Linda was that person. I also learned, in the years to come, that having a warm 'mother figure' in the office had a soothing effect on staff and students alike.

Lord of the Harvest

I hate that sense that everyone is looking at me at the party because I'm not talking to anyone. Of course, no one is looking, but that lonely, creeping feeling in one's heart is never nice.

As I worked alone in YD, my answer for the loneliness creep was to pray.

Around this time, the Lord carved into the flesh of my heart this verse: 'Pray ye therefore the Lord of the harvest, that he will send forth labourers into his harvest' (Matt 9:35, KJV).

I remember preaching on 'The Rotting Harvest' at a Youth for Christ 'Youth Happening', where I saw a huge response. I challenged them to pray every day for a month, 'I will go anywhere, do anything, give anything, when you tell me.'

A guy who responded at that program wrote to me, saying he was scared the Lord would send him to Africa if he prayed this prayer. He took up the challenge to pray. Guess where he ended up? Africa – and he loved it!

Yet, there was another reason I was hanging onto this verse. I was desperate for someone to work with me. By now it was 1984. I had clocked up six years on the speedo since I'd started YD – and still no one came to join me. When I look at my 1984 journal, I see that I was praying for a workmate in January, August, November and December – and so it went on into 1985. Man's best friend may be a dog, but a Christian worker's best friend is the one he or she works with.

You want to know something peculiar? On Wednesday June 20, 1984, our son Jamie came to the Lord. Little did I know that this little primary-school-aged child was to come and start work in YD in the early 2000s. So, while I was praying and claiming this verse about the harvest, the Lord was also preparing an answer for my prayer – to come to fruition eighteen years later.

During this period, the Lord gave us many dedicated volunteers. To this day, I rejoice in how they helped keep me going. Yet I longed for a soulmate who would work with me, side by side and heart by heart.

I prayed and prayed. Nothing was happening, even after two years of praying. I remember the board saying, 'There's only so much cash in the Christian pool, so we shouldn't expect much.' I often think of that when I consider how we eventually rose to twenty-five staff.

Despite my loneliness, my observation has been the Lord always provided the personnel we needed at any given time.

Only Luke is with me …
2 Timothy 4:11a NIV

Three Possibilities

During our years at Bible college, they used to hold an annual picnic up in the Yarra Valley. For many, there was great excitement around this event; it was the time the male students made their move on the girl they had been thinking about all year!

To mix up the day, the college held running races. One year, I entered the 800-metre race, as I fancied myself as a bit of a middle-distance runner.

Picture this: I'm on the last lap and I hit the front, with no training. The crowd is cheering, and a commentator is screaming out over the loudspeaker system, 'Coyle's hit the front.' It's a euphoric moment – and it's going to last about as long as a bee's whisker. With around a hundred metres to go, my roommate comes level with me. We run neck and neck for the last hundred metres. I feel as if my chest is going to cave in, and they'll have to erect a statue on that spot with the epitaph, 'Coyle died here.'

I lost.

To add insult to injury, they then rang the ambulance to come and get me. I was so exhausted, I collapsed like a deflated balloon on the track. I still remember that feeling of gasping for air but not being able to suck enough in to return my breathing to normal. The ambos pumped oxygen into me and gradually my breathing settled. There had been a moment of panic, where I wondered if my breathing would actually return to normal.

Difficult times in ministry can leave you feeling total exhaustion in your spirit. There are times when you think that life will never return to normal. The only problem is, there is no ambo waiting with the special oxygen for life and ministries during hard times.

I have often said that there are three possible reasons hard times come knocking.

Number one: the Lord is testing you. That can be like walking up a cliff face, backwards.

Number two: you inflict pain on yourself by decisions you made in self-interest.

Number three: the devil is taking a big swing at you. If you poke him in the eye by trying to win back those who follow him, we shouldn't be surprised that he will try and take us out.

The bottom line? The source of hard times in our lives has to be one of these three: God, self or the devil.

Give me some advice. Give me some counsel. What would you say to me about the source of my hardship after reading these journal entries?

From July 19:

'The last few weeks have brought enormous pressure ...'

'The schools ministry has taken a battering. Hadfield High was a shocker because of the incredible opposition from the students. Baxter Tech was cancelled due to incredible opposition from the school staff.'

'My own personal health has been off.'

'I am facing a deep relationship hassle.'

'My overall program is swamping me ... the whole YD work I feel in myself as well as my being is open to question. Thoughts like "I shouldn't go on", which I never normally entertain, come firing in on me. The finances are just holding their head above water ... How much is this opposition from Satan? Is the Lord trying to tell me something? I pray constantly for another worker, but none comes.'

And on July 30:

'I have been in much despair over the past few days.'

This had become an 'I can't breathe' moment in my ministry. It felt like falling without a parachute, knowing that the ground was rushing to embrace me.

I am not alone in feeling such things in ministry. I think of Moses, Jonah and Elijah in particular, who all basically said to the Lord, 'Take me home, I've had enough!'

Yet here I am, many years later, somehow having survived those suffocating moments of ministry.

It's not just ministry that can drain life. Personal issues have just as much capacity to weaken resolve to keep trusting. In actual fact, we have all known those 'I can't go on' moments. It maybe through a small group that is more interested in the specials at Coles than the Scriptures. It could be a child whose temperamental make-up resembles a Tyrannosaurus Rex, or a church whose appreciation of you is as deep as a cat's saucer of milk. All these trials, and more, suffocate the life out of us.

My experience has taught me there is an end to these moments; those moments where you feel life is holding its hand over your mouth and nose. Just surviving these times is a miracle.

Can I encourage you to take comfort in the knowledge that the Lord is there? When we are guessing at the source of our hardship, we need to stop guessing and simply remember – he is there.

He means it when he says,

I will never you leave you nor forsake you.
Hebrews 13:5 (ESV)

An Apparition

The mum's voice asked over the phone, 'Did you speak on séances at Presbyterian Ladies College?' I had no idea what was coming. Was I going to be attacked, questioned, or even reported?

This lady wanted to come and talk to me. Out came an incredible story of how she and her husband, with another couple, had held a séance downstairs in their home. Upstairs was their young daughter in her bedroom. They heard screaming and found their daughter out of her bed and cowering in a corner. The young girl told her mum and dad she had seen an old woman's face in the room, and it had generated unbelievable terror. The tale continued with more weird happenings.

This non-Christian woman had come to see me out of desperation and fear.

What would you have done?

Around the same time, I ran a week-long mission at Wantirna High School. I spoke on Satan and séances. A couple of kids had been in our program the day before and I had chucked them out for bad behaviour. So, what did they do? They thought, 'We'll have a séance while he's talking about it.' They clearly thought, in some twisted way, that this would get back at me.

I knew nothing about it until the school rang me that night and told me the mission was closed down. When the students who had caused me problems held their séance, they saw something supernaturally awful. It sent one of them into a trance. At first, they couldn't drag him out of the stupor he had gone into. They had to walk that student around the school oval for an hour to get him out of it. I was blamed for it.

What would you have done?

Coincidently – or not so coincidentally, as we really know – two other factors were weighing on us. Our finances were moving to a crisis point, and every time I went away at least one of the kids got sick.

What would you have done?

Pam said to me, 'Maybe the devil is attacking us.'

I was imagining what would happen if the media got hold of the Wantirna student trance situation. YD would be dead in the water.

So, what *did* we do?

In all these situations, we prayed – and simply resisted Satan.

The result was that the lady with the child, who was troubled, had no more occurrences of weird happenings. The Wantirna situation evaporated into nothing. The money poured in and the kids stopped getting sick while I was away.

Paul's words are true:

We wrestle not against flesh and blood ...

Ephesians 6:12 (KJV)

'What Have I Done?'

It was a Saturday morning in 1984 and the farmhouse in which we were living on my father-in-law's farm had grass so high, I almost expected leopards to come prowling out at any moment.

Maybe a little writer's license there – but the lawn certainly did need a mow. If we were to show appreciation for the in-laws putting us up while our new house was being built, the least I could do was mow the grass using Pam's dad's ride-on lawnmower.

Jamie was five years old at the time and seeing his dad using the ride-on mower excited him, so I pulled him up onto my lap. In a moment that is frozen in my memory, I moved him to sit on the bonnet of the mower. I turned the mower right, and he fell off to the left. His arm went under the mower.

It still stings me unbelievably to recall what followed. Jamie's left hand could best be described as mangled. In horror, I looked and thought I had amputated my son's hand. My body and mind went numb.

Pam, who is immensely calm in crisis, arrived and held Jamie's arm and what remained of his hand in a bloodied towel as we raced to Lilydale Hospital. I remember banging the steering wheel of our Toyota Corona and saying, 'What have I done?' Jamie was crying, asking 'Will I be able to ride my BMX?'

Two hospitals in a row couldn't handle the situation and referred us on eventually to the Austin Hospital, one of the large hospitals in Melbourne.

The doctor who was to operate had a boy the same age as Jamie. I remember buckling at the knees when I had to sign a form to say he could amputate Jamie's hand.

Amazingly, there still remained an artery attached to Jamie's damaged hand even though around seventy millimetres of bone had been taken out of his wrist. So here was the challenge. We have what remained of a live hand, but it was unattached to Jamie's arm by bone. It was alive only via the artery.

For six weeks, Jamie was in hospital while the doctors wondered what to do. Christians all over Australia had found out what had happened and were praying. Then a miracle happened. The gap of bone closed. The splintered bone from the arm grew back to connect to the hand.

Now, I am not a medico. But we were told that bones only grow when the growth points at the end of the bone are there. Jamie had lost his via the accident. The doctor's explanation for this miraculous growth? 'Isn't nature wonderful!' Our explanation differed slightly: 'God answers prayers in miraculous ways.'

Of course, many operations ensued to clean and fix things up. Jamie lost a finger, but gained enough use of his hand that he can play the guitar left-handed. It was a miracle.

The impact on our family was huge. My hair went grey overnight. Pam did countless doctor's visits, and we had many trips to hospitals for operations. For the family, including the girls, it drove us closer to Jesus than we had ever experienced before.

Suffering is often the crucible by which intimacy comes, both with God and with his people.

No One To Dance with

I don't like people looking over my shoulder, let alone reading my journal over my shoulder. It's rude.

But, at no extra expense, have a peak at these 1985 journal entries and feel my loneliness and pain as I longed for someone to work with me after eight-and-a-half years by myself in YD.

> January 2: 'Continue to grant me that burden to pray for more harvesters for the field ...'
>
> August 2: 'I continue to pray the Lord will raise up another worker ...'
>
> October 30: 'I continue to long for the Lord to open up the way for someone to come in fulltime in YD.'
>
> December 31: 'I long over the next twelve months to pray more consistently for Australia and for the Lord to raise up workers for YD.'

It wasn't until 1986 that the Lord answered my prayers. The Lord gradually released a steady stream of workers to come to YD. I look back and gape in awe at his ultimate provision.

I didn't know if anyone would ever come on staff. I rubbed shoulders in those days with men whom I thought (and prayed) would come into the work. Geoff Leslie, Craig Broman, Tim Costello, Jeff Pugh, Martin and Andrew Boutros are names you may not know, but take it from me they all had great hearts for Jesus and a wealth of talent to boot. All went into ministry – but not with YD.

I was pleased for them and for the many others who were to become strategic in the Lord's plans. Yet I was as alone as the rejected nerd waiting for a girl to come and ask him for a dance. I felt the dance would never come.

Loneliness in ministry is soul destroying. One's sense of significance is easily crushed by loneliness. One's sense of worth can be reduced to ashes. Eight-and-a-half years of loneliness is more than a sip of loneliness – it's a whole keg full.

As David prayed (and I love the old King James rendering of this verse):

Why art thou cast down, O my soul? And why art thou disquieted
in me? Hope thou in God: for I shall yet praise him
for the help of his countenance.
Psalm 42:5 KJV

In my lonely moments, I clung to God. The lessons of my lonely moments as a teenager had trained me. I hoped in God and 'the help of his countenance.' He is a refuge for the lonely, particularly when all human help can't lift you up.

1986: Growth Begins

I have a confession: I like 'whodunnit' movies. I like to get myself into 'whodunnit' mode. 'Hmmm, why did he look sideways? Why did he drop that envelope?' I go looking for clues and try to pick the end of the movie.

1986 was the year that the Lord dropped clues all over the place. On reflection, I think, 'How dense am I?' (Don't answer that!)

Up until this time YD was a one-man band. It was just Rob Coyle, working in schools and preaching everywhere. This was the year that brought change.

Here are the clues that were dropped, which dramatically reshaped the image of YD.

First, the YD board embraced the concept of linking schools with the local church. This was a long way from the original operation, where, in conjunction with local ISCF groups, Christian kids would get me to come in and do my thing.

The rationale for the change was ministry sustainability. Outreach work in a school could potentially last longer if owned by a church rather than a lunchtime group run by Christian students. These students, of course, moved on once they had finished Year 12. As a result, Christian groups would fold, because frequently there were no student leaders for the next year. If a church owned the outreach in a school, it would potentially become more sustainable.

We eventually came to the point where we said we would not work in a school unless a local church owned that ministry. I have since seen churches invest over twenty years of time in local schools.

The board's decision was a paradigm shift, and we didn't realise it would have a massive impact on YD; but more about that later.

Second, we created a three-day-a-week internship program that would run for twelve months. It had such modest beginnings, but was to eventually fertilise YD to the point where new staff were coming in on a yearly basis.

Third, I let go of eldership at my local church. Resigning from eldership was painful, as I had enjoyed it immensely, but it freed up more time for me.

Fourth, our first YD staff member, Greg McCracken, came on board. By the end of the year, I also had two interns lined up for 1987: Denise Hyland and Mike Muldoon.

I am stunned as I reflect back on 1986. I think it was the Lord unleashing answers to the prayers of my lonely, broken 1985 heart.

We have a great God who won't ignore the cries of our heart.

He heals the broken-hearted and binds up their wounds.
Psalm 147:3 NIV

A Lesson Learned

'Ministry would be perfect if there were no people involved!'

So said one of my friends. I've often joked over this statement with pastors who are struggling with people in their church.

As I prayed for staff to come on board, I didn't realise I was also asking the Lord to challenge me in how I led a team.

The Lord graciously helped me to stumble onto the best way forward regarding staff. At first, I couldn't see it. There it was, as plain as Mount Everest in front of me, but thick-as-a-brick Rob took a while to see that Everest. I was missing a staff selection principle. I had one staff person, Greg McCracken, but I still hadn't figured out the key to gaining new staff.

The principle was, select your key staff from those you have intimately invested your life in.

I had been buying up shares in the lives of our two interns, Michael and Denise. We had prayed together, learned together and ministered together, and I had grown to perceive the true nature of their hearts. They had good hearts. They would make excellent staff – and eventually, that's what they became.

I have made some monumental blunders with staff. But placing a requirement on staff to do internships for one to two years has saved me and my team a lot of pain. When you work with a person for a year or so, you get a pretty good idea of what they are like – and, just as importantly, what you are like.

So they went and saw where he [Jesus] was staying, and they spent the day with him.

John 1:39 NIV

North Ringwood

I love North Ringwood, Victoria. It's leafy, undulating, quiet and relaxed. Its neighbouring suburbs, literally three minutes' drive from our house, are semi-rural. There, you will find five- and ten-acre lots with rolling hills and tall gum trees. The Yarra River is nearby. There is a delightful, varied bird population, and goats, sheep and horses scattered around the local landscape. If I sound like the local real estate agent, it's just because Pam and I loved where the Lord had put us for this season.

After Dad's death, Mum moved to Panton Hills, another outer eastern Melbourne suburb, with my sister, Zayda. Eventually, Mum moved back to North Ringwood and built a fabulous double-story house in a quiet court. Downstairs was a rumpus room, two bedrooms and a bathroom.

At the end of November 1986, Mum offered the downstairs section of her house for a YD office, rent free. She would live upstairs. On January 12, 1987, we moved in. It was an incredible provision. And it was only a goat's breath from our place. The surroundings were delightful. It was the Lord's provision.

For some reason, I tended not to think of gifts from my parents as provision from the Lord. Silly, I know, but I fell into thinking that that's what parents are meant to do. Perhaps you can relate. But this was the Lord's way of looking after us, big time. There were no bills for electricity, water or rates, and no rent. My Mum covered them all.

In the lead up to the shift of office, a couple of important decisions were made – the kind you look back on and think, 'What if we hadn't decided that?'

The biggest was the commencement of our internship program at YD. Peter Atkinson, whom I had come to know quite well through ministry in Tassie during my OAC days, dreamed with me of a 'hands-on internship program.' He talked of one in Tassie, while I talked of one in Victoria. There are times when fellow dreamers hold you up to the possibility of a dream fulfilled. Have you got a dream?

I buried myself in the Gospels and asked myself, 'How did Jesus disciple people?' I became convinced that the way forward was to touch the head (biblical input), the hands (gift development) and the heart (one's walk with Jesus).

My journal reveals that the YD board was, in September of 1986, divided on the internship concept. Pam was unsettled about it still in October. Finally, however, it was embraced late on October 26.

Personally, I was still nervous about the step at the end of that year. I speculate now about what would have happened if I'd given into fear. There would have been no Denise, who still serves with YD, and no Michael, who gave us five years' service. There wouldn't have been the provision of around fifty staff through internship. We wouldn't have reached seventy percent of the schools we reached. We wouldn't have seen a host of incredible opportunities to grow young Christians. I shudder at the thought of us turning our back on that decision.

So there we were in 1987, in Mum's rumpus room with a brick feature wall and apricot carpet: Linda Schaefer (secretary), Denise Hyland and Mike Muldoon (two interns), me and ... and ... our first YD staff member, Greg McCracken.

Here was the beginning of something I'd dreamed of for years: a YD team.

I am so glad we didn't give in to fear. Don't let fear stop you from risky obedience. Don't give in.

Even though I walk through the darkest valley, I will fear no evil.
Psalm 23:4a NIV

Wagons Ho

Picture a circle of old canvas-covered wagons. A stray dog lifts its sleepy head at a coyote's call while the horses, tied to a rope between two old, gnarly trees, munch away on some parched grass. Smoke from a fire drifts gently up into the clear, starry sky. Around the fire, there's a large gathering of folk who dream of a better life in the West.

What makes you stare at this gathering is the steady gaze of all upon one man who stands among them, speaking with an unusual authority. He is sharing the gospel.

The preaching of the gospel to folk travelling westward in the States was the go in those days. When this 'Go West' movement was in full flight, the

Lord used this method of campsite evangelistic meetings to great effect. When the movement West faded, so did the methodology.

Over the years, I have seen churches and parachurch groups become blind to the fact that a certain method is dead in the water. They confuse the methodology with theology and will die for the methodology, thinking it is unchangeable. They'll defend it as though they are dying for the truth of the resurrection.

One of my greatest fears in YD had been that we would become wedded to a methodology in schools that we were not prepared to change because 'that's the way we've always done it.'

When a method is stone dead, the challenge is to find what to put in its place rather than continuing to justify its existence.

There was a time when sketch board evangelism worked. It is now buried, along with my sketch board, in the YD cemetery of old methods.

For a period of time, we ran what we called 'clubs' (I cringe at that name now). The idea was to have a place where kids from schools could come, have fun and hear the gospel, while also providing a stepping stone into youth group and church. At the same time, we ran camps during the year, to which these students were invited.

My body aches even now as I think of the horse-riding camps, the goldrush camps (an excuse to play bush games), the watery weekends (water, water and water) – and so it went on. We saw truckloads of teens trust Jesus at these camps. Andrew and Linda Boutros and Geoff Leslie were an incredible help when this methodology was in full swing.

But the method died, and we moved on.

It's what makes ministry exciting, finding out what is the next method the Lord wants to use.

From 1987 on, the methods we were using started to drift and the model of local church involvement in schools arrived. They were exciting times.

What method is God using with you now? Enjoy the season until he changes it again. But don't hang onto something just because that's the way it's 'always been done.'

Neither do people pour new wine into old wine skins ...
Matthew 9:17a NIV

Student Focus Gains Wings

If you are claustrophobic, you'll hate it. If you don't like being touched, you'll dread it! If peculiar smells make your stomach turn, you'll (almost) heave! If loud noises, like a pack of chimpanzees on Red Bull, annoy you, you'll avoid it!

What am I describing? A walk down a secondary-school corridor as the students are let loose for lunch.

It's a montage of bags, books, sandwiches, potato chips, flailing limbs, noisy mouths and restless teenage hormones.

I have walked down hundreds of school corridors, and I love it. Maybe it's the sense of life that ricochets off those lockers, walls, windows and dirty stained floors. My favourite corridor is at Norwood Secondary College in North Ringwood, Victoria. I started going to this school's lunchtime programs as far back as 1974. I lived in North Ringwood, so it has a special place in my heart.

In the eight-and-a-half years I was by myself in YD, I would rock up at schools on a Monday lunchtime, do my thing, go home and return the next lunchtime, and so on, till Friday. Sometimes, I would come in the week before and do surveys in the schoolyard with students. This would be an opportunity to ask the kids to come the following week to the lunchtime program. I had done several of these style missions at Norwood.

In my diary, I notice that the name 'Student Focus' first appears in connection with Norwood. The name came from one of our YD board members, John Charlton, who ran an outreach program called Student Focus at Doncaster High School. John allowed us to pinch the name for our weekly school programs.

Student Focus was kind of like rubbing a dirty old rock and discovering you had been carrying a diamond around. We had no idea that the Student Focus program for Years 7 and 8 would turn out to be a precious gem.

What was Student Focus? A mate of mine, Ian Purse, had been running games in Bayswater Secondary College at lunchtime and getting great regular numbers. I tried it at Norwood and found that kids came regularly. After a period of time I added a devotional relevant to young people, and the whole Student Focus concept gained wings and started to take off. I was told by the school (which had a junior and senior lunchtime) I could only run it at junior high lunchtimes.

This was a God thing. Why? Because this style, we later discovered, only worked with junior levels. If the seniors came in (our later observations proved) they would have wrecked it and the concept would have never got off the runway.

This taught me that there is nothing wrong with using trial and error to see what works.

> **For my thoughts are not your thoughts, neither are**
> **your ways my ways,' declares the LORD.**
> Isaiah 55:8 NIV

Tuna Mornay

Tuna mornay. I can hardly write the words. They stick in my throat and on the end of my computer tablet as I write. This very day, we sang 'Happy Birthday' to our grandson Sunny, and he told us he is having tuna mornay as a treat for dinner. If I'm ever being tortured, my captors would only need to threaten me with a force-feeding of tuna mornay to get whatever information they need.

No one in their right mind orders a meal that they find as unpalatable as a can of dog food. Tuna mornay tastes like that to me.

My experience of working alone for eight-and-a-half years had scarred me like a tuna mornay banquet. There was no way I wanted to return to those days. Greg, our first YD staff member, had moved on after eighteen months. Our two interns, Michael and Denise, now into their second year at YD, were wrestling through what their futures would be. Would they stay?

That mornay taste started to loom as a very real possibility. I'd be alone again.

This possibility was magnified by other pressures in my life. I struggled with waves of melancholy. They swept over my life like an incoming tide, and I felt I was drowning under YD financial pressures and the possibility of working by myself again in the coming year. The year 1988 felt like someone was holding my head under water and I could get no air. Ever felt that?

Maybe this was why earlier in that year, the chairman of the board, Eric

Price, had wondered out loud whether I should consider a youth pastor position at our church, Ringwood Brethren.

Then two other members of the board, Tim Costello and Bruce Saward, suggested an amalgamation with Youth for Christ. My brother Paul suggested the same a few months later. It made me feel as if YD was an ocean liner named *Titanic*.

What would you have done?

The Lord stepped in with two significant events.

First, he clearly called Denise and Michael, after a period of uncertainty, to YD. This was to bin the tuna mornay feeling forever. I was never a solitary staff member again.

Second, through my mum, I was given $1,000 to enable us to take twelve weeks of long-service leave.

Pam, the kids and I went on a twelve-week holiday. I recovered from being mentally hammered. The family never forgot that particular holiday. For me personally, this time out restored perspective and my sense of calling.

Even though we were close to extinction the next year, I could face it.

All at once an angel touched him and said, 'Get up and eat'. He looked around and there by his head was a cake of bread baked over hot coals, and a jar of water. He ate and drank and then lay down again.

1 Kings 19:5b, 6 NIV

Sometimes we just don't realise that, like Elijah, we need a good sleep and break to restore perspective.

Had this break not come, I really wonder if I would have been able to continue leading YD. It was the Lord's cake and water for me – a little miracle.

Here's a ministry tip I've found invaluable in facing difficulty, melancholy and pressure: never, never neglect your Sabbath or your yearly holidays.

Extinction

Whatever happened to Craven A cigarettes, the Leyland P76 and Banana Crème ice-creams? I know you've never heard of them – they are extinct.

In 1989, we were on the verge of extinction. We were on the edge of 'Whatever happened to Youth Dimension?'

On May 2, there was $700 in the bank to keep us running. On July 25, we sunk as low as $150. On Friday July 28, I discovered that the money we had wasn't sufficient to pay the staff on Monday. Five hundred dollars came in over the weekend, and we lived for yet another day.

This was the story for all of 1989 and into 1990. What became very precious to me at that time was that part of the Lord's prayer, 'Give us this day our daily bread.'

As a family, we lived hand-to-mouth just like YD, as did the other staff, yet we never lacked.

On July 27, I wrote in my diary a prayer: 'Lord, our personal support is nowhere … we are in danger of draining the funds completely. Lord, you are Jehovah Jireh and without you stepping in again … our ministry is lost.'

All that year, the Lord stepped in again and again. We had special board meetings. We moved from a policy of not telling people our financial needs to informing them. It's fascinating to note that nothing changed. We continued to live on the edge of extinction, only to be saved repeatedly by timely, small gifts.

The Lord was teaching us that he will supply daily, that this was his ministry and that he could close it at any time he wanted to. Have you ever thought that the Lord could close whatever ministry you have? It's never our ministry; it's always his.

So Abraham called that place The LORD Will Provide.

Genesis 22:14a NIV

1990 – Another Decade

In 1989, I was learning how to spell 'extinction' as we lurched from one financial crisis to another. We were stumbling around like a drunkard at midnight, dressed in black, walking down the freeway. I felt as though it was only a matter of time before we met with a nasty road accident.

So, what did Bert Guy, our new treasurer, put to the board on May 26, 1990? He suggested we put the YD staff salary on a similar level to the Baptist Union of Victoria's salary pay line. This would almost double our salary from $17,000 to $30,000 – for me as director, $33,000. I don't think I'd heard anything more insane in all my years on the YD board. It defied, even laughed at, human logic.

I remember sitting in the board meeting and thinking, 'If we do this we'll run out of money in a month.' I said that out loud in the meeting. Bert stood firm, however, insisting that what staff were being paid was wrong and that a labourer was worthy of his or her hire. So the change was made.

By the next month, we had run out of money. Bert personally made up the shortfall every month, and within a short period of time the money was regularly coming in. It was another miracle. You've got to love people with an insane faith, who dare to believe what the Lord has told them. I have never forgotten Bert's generosity, care and faith and the sense of worth he gave people in ministry.

I often forget this, that God speaks through his people to us. For me, in so many ways, the body of Christ corrects, encourages or – in this case – affirms me. It is the Lord's way of saying, 'I'm with you.'

There have been many times since 1990 that YD has been on the edge of extinction. Although it can stretch faith to doubt and bring sleepless nights, I love it. I love an insane faith that says, 'Do it, Lord.'

I love it when life has no backup plan and you are in freefall, utterly dependent on the Lord to catch you. I do think the Lord has a sense of humour, because as I write this all of our kids, who are married with kids, are living in the same way in their own ministries. They likewise live in freefall, trusting God for daily provision.

It's exciting waiting for God to catch you.

He will cover you with his feathers, and under his wings you will find refuge;
his faithfulness will be your shield and rampart.

Psalm 91:4 NIV

Friends

I can't explain it, but whenever I was away from home doing ministry, with around twenty-four hours to go, a button of home anticipation would be pressed inside of me. As soon as that button was pressed, a feeling of excitement built and the smile on my face said, 'It's time to go home to Pam and the kids.'

I travelled to South Australia, New South Wales, Queensland and Western Australia. I would be away for around a week at a time. My program would consist of coaching schools workers, running training, preaching in churches and building on new contacts I had made.

I built some wonderful relationships in Western Australia in around ten years of ministry there. The key folks I connected with in that area were Lyn and Tam Devlin, Bruce and Glenys Eagles (plus family) and Ric and Ais Maxwell. They would come out to the Perth airport to say goodbye to me.

On one visit very early in my ministry, I was in a stupid but excited mood about going home. I was at the airport with these friends, saying goodbye and trying to entertain them. I told them I had to go to the loo, and I started waving like a five-year-old on stage to his mum in the audience as I disappeared into the toilets.

When I got inside, I thought to myself, 'What's that lady doing in the men's toilets? … And that lady?' And then it dawned on me, 'I'm in the ladies'!'

I'll leave it to your imagination as to what kind of response I received when I walked out of the ladies' toilets to see my West Australian friends in fits.

These dear people not only helped open up numerous preaching opportunities for me but were outstanding Christian friends who embraced me as part of their families.

It was an incredible answer to prayer. I had been praying for six months before my first trip west for the Lord to show me whether he wanted YD to go interstate. These preaching trips provided occasions to talk about schools outreach. My preaching was a way of opening up opportunities to talk to churches about the potential of working in schools. It led to YD being invited to do schools work in Western Australia.

My travelling gave me many precious times of friendship. What an incredible gift.

To my dear friend Gaius, whom I love in the truth.
3 John 1:1 NIV

Sell the Cattle

Harry Ironside was a great Bible teacher who lectured at the Moody Bible Institute in the USA. He prayed this prayer at a time when the Institute was in financial crisis. 'Lord you own the cattle on a thousand hills. Sell some.' Incredibly, before 12 pm that very day, a Texan walked into the Institute with a gift that saved the day. The money came from the proceeds of the cattle he had sold!

This story really impressed me. In 1990, as we faced financial crisis after financial crisis, I remember praying, 'Lord, you did it for Harry Ironside. Do it for us; sell some cattle.'

As the Lord is my witness, two days later we received a gift from a farmer friend who had been fattening cattle to sell for missions. It was one of those 'pinch me, I don't believe this is real' moments. It encouraged me so much to pray and pray.

The Lord gave YD not only money, but people.

On November 29, 1990, someone literally walked off the street into our offices. I thought, 'Who the hang is this guy?' He was stocky, confident, an aircraft mechanic and had been through Bible college. He wanted to know about coming on staff, so we told him he had to do a twelve-month internship, even though he had done Bible college. Initially, I was deeply suspicious. My experience had been in the past that cold-contact types who wanted to come on staff were highly unusual people.

Sometimes, you just don't recognise a gift from the Lord when it comes. Lindsay (Lins) Tunbridge, who came in that day, turned out to be one of the most valuable staff members, ever.

In 1990 we had one intern, Steve Carr, and in 1991 we leapt to three: Celia Larkin, Christ Danes and Lindsay Tunbridge. The Lord was clearly cementing internship into the YD landscape.

Meanwhile, I was dreaming a dream about our weekly lunchtime school programs.

Could we possibly reach 100 schools by 1995?

Could we buy an office building for $600,000?

Could I grow the staff to fifteen or even twenty?

I look back and smirk. I was almost a split personality, one day crying out to the Lord, 'Save YD', the next day dreaming what seemed impossible dreams.

Can I ask suggest something to you? If you're a cautious type, learn to keep your mouth shut around dreamers, particularly those with impossible dreams. Listen first before even contemplating coming out with the pessimism. There are enough people out there in Wet Blanket Land, dampening dreamers.

**The tongue has the power of life and death,
and those who love it will eat its fruit.**
Proverbs18:21 NIV

The Snare

I learned something obvious in the early 90s. Smarties are different colours!

By now there were seven staff on the YD team, plus a couple of voluntary workers. They were like Smarties, all different colours. We were all very different in age, temperament, spirituality and in the baggage we carried. I was learning that each person has a unique colour, requiring a unique approach.

Having been virtually by myself for nearly nine years, I found myself around the twelve-year mark on a learning curve that was so steep, it was past perpendicular. As I look back at this period of time, I can see that I was labouring to come to grips with leadership. It was as much about the Lord teaching me to lead as me leading this little band.

Events happened during that year, 1991, that were so difficult I have not experienced them since. The Lord had the fire turned up to blistering hot on Rob Coyle's leadership. In many instances I melted instead of standing firm, and the Lord made me resit many of these searching tests again and again.

On top of people's personal issues, growth issues were emerging. Our school work was growing. I was preaching all over the place. I was overseeing the internship program. I was struggling with my local church. We were frequently in financial crisis, and I was battling some form of depression.

I'll let you work out how I was going as a dad and husband.

When you are a born people pleaser and a fear-prone person, confrontation feels as challenging as having to climb Mount Everest naked. Yet this was the mountain the Lord wanted me to climb. I learned very quickly that if I don't face necessary confrontation, things get worse, not better.

I remember learning this verse from Proverbs: 'Fear of man will prove to be a snare, but whoever trusts in the Lord is kept safe' (Prov 29:25 NIV). This was a year of the snare. Eventually I got the message: when you avoid them rather than face them, people problems don't go away.

I have been asked many times, 'How have you lasted over forty years in ministry?' For me, time with the Lord was the key. Without it, my struggle with confrontation could have put me out of ministry.

On Monday March 18, 1991, I wrote in my diary:

> Lord, I'm not going to make it unless I can claim your all-sufficient grace. I have become aware of the need to feed my soul more. I am aware the summer period will end soon … it will be harder to rise in the morning and my time with you, Lord, will be under even greater pressure. Lord grant me continuing resolve to make time with you each day …

There is nothing special about me – or you, for that matter. But there is something special about spending time with God. Time alone with God is a key to lasting in ministry.

Very early in the morning, while it was still dark, Jesus got up, left the house and went off to a solitary place, where he prayed.

Mark 1:35 NIV

Thick as a Brick

This isn't pretty. In fact, it's about as ugly as the bottom of a food waste bin. This is the ugly side of me wrestling with unanswered prayer.

I write my prayers. On December 1, 1992, I wrote:

> I have all year wrestled in prayer over four to five main issues and hit a brick wall. It has even eaten at me sometimes. It has frustrated me. I have wondered and asked, 'Why?'

> Is my love for the Lord hinging on me getting my way with YD? If my quality of ministry suffered, would I spit the dummy and surrender my love for you, Lord?

Prayer can be frustrating. Sometimes the Lord just won't co-operate!

What had I been praying about, all 1992?

I had been praying for a new office, as we had run out of space at Mum's. I had been asking for three to five interns, for an administrator, and for a change in the board, as it had been bruised by the painful events of the previous year.

This is what I wrote, with clenched mouth and gritted teeth, on December 1:

> … no new office, no administrator, two possible interns and the board is struggling.

Do we fail to recognise the Lord's answers to prayer because he puts a different slant on his answer? Have you ever kept praying, even though the Lord has already answered?

Listen to an example of this in my life. We didn't get a new office. But we did get a renovated garage at Mum's place. It gave us the extra space we needed.

We didn't get a paid administrator. But we did increase our receptionist Linda's days of work from three to five, which meant Linda could do our administration. And a retired plumber, Ric Batchelor, volunteered to help with property and office maintenance, which was another part of the administration role we needed.

By January 1, 1993, we had three interns and two great new board members, Andree Shepherd and Wayne Collins. I look back now and say, 'I'm thick!' How could I have not seen God's answer to the prayers I had offered for our needs?

Maybe the Lord has answered one of your prayers and you don't know it. I hope you are not as thick as I was.

Do not be anxious about anything, but in every situation, by prayer and petition, with thanksgiving, present your requests to God.
Philippians 4:6 NIV

Dots

Random ... random ... random ... yet the dots joined.

I often ask a couple how they met, and frequently it's through some random set of circumstances. Later in life they look back and say, 'If we hadn't gone to that footy match, that wedding, that friend's place for dinner, we may not have ended up together.' They realise that the Lord joined the dots together and they were brought together by him.

The year 1992 was full of random and joined dots. I spoke at Heathmont Baptist early that year and moved to that church in early 1993. Coincidental?

Kim, our eldest, had entered a relationship with her boyfriend. Michael Miatke, her future husband, strolled into our office in February, wanting to help. At the time, Pam and I were praying for Kim's future partner. Michael and Kim met in December 1992 and became an item in Feb 1993, ten months after Michael had entered the YD office. Coincidental?

I met and chatted to a lady called Lyn Devlin in Perth. Lyn ended up organising our schools work in Western Australia for ten years. Coincidental?

Of course, coincidence isn't the word. The right words are, 'The sovereign hand of God.'

After a tumultuous 1991, 1992 was a year I look back on and say, 'Wow, the Lord's hand was on us.' By the end of the year, YD had broken into Tasmania, South Australia and Western Australia to commence schools work with local churches. We were in thirty-five schools running weekly lunchtime programs – amazing, considering the concept of weekly lunchtime programs was just over two years old.

On top of this, our summer outreach, now called Solid Rock Café, had bolted to sixteen locations, with teams in four states. We had five hundred and eighty at our Victorian commissioning service and three hundred at an afternoon music service before the commissioning service!

I was running a weekly program in Norwood Secondary College, with over sixty coming along.

Lindsay Tunbridge was working incredibly hard on our interstate work. Celia Larkin was assisting our schools work on a part-time basis. Denise was being Denise and holding the details together, while Lins and I ran around talking about schools outreach to everyone.

I look back on this year, where everything we touched turned to gold, with fond memories. It was the sovereign hand of God. 'Random' meetings, people, visits, phone calls – the Lord just joined the dots. Finance was steady with no crisis. All was incredibly good.

If there is one fact of life I've learned, it's to never despise the random moments of life. Ever met someone randomly and thought, 'I'll never see them again?' You may not, but remember the great joiner of dots, our sovereign God, has the big picture.

A lady came up to me the other day and said 'Rob Coyle! I came to the Lord through your ministry at a study camp.' I had no idea who she was, but it made me recognise that I was a dot in the grand scheme of life the Lord had for her. Think about that when you next engage in conversation with the lady serving you coffee in that little café you go to around the corner. Nothing is insignificant.

If I had to choose a favourite year of ministry, 1992 would go close to it. But every year has its dots, and the shadow of the hand of God on it. Over this year, he will be connecting the dots for you.

Let Go

Youth Dimension was taking off. There were new growth shoots everywhere. How exciting is it when you see the Lord creating growth in your life? This was happening with us in YD.

Our summer outreach, Solid Rock, was in its prime. There were nearly two hundred people who came to a week-long training course in evangelism. Alongside the training in Victoria, we had training courses in Tassie and Western Australia for people who wanted to do summer outreach in those states.

In 1993, our schools work was exploding interstate. Here's an example. In our lunchtime programs in Perth, Belridge Secondary School had a hundred and fifty attending, while Como Secondary School had a hundred and twenty. Lyn Devlin was being paid by us for one day a week in Perth but giving us many more hours. She was an incredible provision.

Lins, Denise, our newest staff member Mandy Cocking (nee Stark) and I were travelling each term to Sydney, to the north coast of Tassie, to Perth and to Adelaide to support the church workers who had embraced our program. We had so much work and it was incredibly exciting. YD was buzzing.

We had prayed for a vehicle, a photocopier and a treasurer for finance, and all were provided. We were flying. Lindsay and I were preaching everywhere, and the Lord was graciously blessing us. We did a camp in Sydney and eighty-three out of a hundred and twenty-one responded!

It was like we were on an intravenous drip of fertilizer.

Then the Lord hammered me with a heart-rending lesson.

On October 26, 1995, I had an interesting chat to Lins. He had been approached by Youth for Christ to go on staff. Lins then told me he had been approached by two other sources to come and work for them. I was cut.

I look back and wonder why I was unhappy. There are a couple of reasons.

First, I had secretly hoped Lindsay would one day take over my role.

Second, staff at YD often became my best buddies, so the thought of losing someone like Lins was grief-inflicting.

Third, how dare someone threaten to take my staff! No, Lins didn't leave, but I was shocked at the idea that someone might take him.

I had to learn to take a kingdom mindset – to value God's kingdom over my own little kingdom. This was the 'let go' lesson the Lord was teaching me. The staff are not mine. They are on loan to YD, by God's grace. Peculiar isn't it – we have to do the same with our kids.

John the Baptist must have had to learn this same lesson that the Lord was teaching me. John had a kingdom mindset.

The next day John was there again with two of his disciples. When he saw Jesus passing by, he said, 'Look, the Lamb of God!' When the two disciples heard him say this, they followed Jesus.

Tick, Tock

Did I need my eyes tested? Was I reading the right words? Pinch me – this had to be a dream. A letter on Ringwood Council letterhead, dated November 14 and addressed to me, contained the following statement:

It is herewith requested that the occupation occurring at the said premises cease by the 15th of December, 1994.

In plain English, 'Youth Dimension, get out of your premises in a month!'

It was at the end of a quiet court in North Ringwood. From the road, the house looked like a single-storey dwelling. The house was made of mottled fawn-and-cream tumbled coach bricks, with a double brick garage out the front. The garden had been beautifully landscaped. It was a lovely house nestled away in a discreet cul-de-sac. This was my mother's house.

It was also the YD office. The downstairs section that YD occupied was at the back of the house. You couldn't see it from the road. But the interns streaming in and out of the garage and the cars parked up and down the court were a giveaway. It was like a sardine picnic in a bottle top. We were absolutely packed with people and busting at the seams.

Stir into the eviction notice the following ingredients: all staff struggling with one or more personal issues; four interns about to leave, to be replaced by eight more; a board not convinced about buying a property (not that we had the money anyway); an identity crisis over whether we existed for outreach to schools or to raise up disciples. Making this recipe really unpalatable was the fact that we had already pushed against many doors to set up new premises, but no door had budged. The council wanted us out.

We felt at YD that we had a split personality. Should our goal be discipleship or evangelism? Or aren't they melded together in life? Can we do both effectively? The choice of where to move to magnified the challenge of clarifying what we existed for. Some felt that YD existed for evangelism, so all we needed was office space for staff. Others felt that we existed also for discipleship and therefore needed a larger space for staff and interns. The eviction notice accelerated the need for a decision about premises. It also intensified the tension around our identity as an organisation.

To make life more interesting, the Liberal government was selling off schools. I dreamed of buying one. There we would be able to activate both dreams: a place for discipleship and a place for staff to reach schools. If we could somehow realise the impossible and secure one of these schools for sale, it would realise a vision I had held since leaving OAC in 1978.

We needed space desperately. Would we rent or buy? Our resources were sparse. What should we do? All year, we had looked at East Ringwood, Norwood and Antonio Park Schools, and at office space in Box Hill and Templestowe, and nothing had worked out for either purchase or rental. Now the pressure to leave was at breaking point. Where were we going to put eight interns (five from interstate), five staff and a couple of voluntary workers? How were we going to pay the rent for any office space? Mum had been giving us our office space rent free, so this was a new financial challenge.

Most importantly, we needed to solve the evangelism–discipleship riddle. Could we keep the two in harmony, or would it be the case that we couldn't serve two masters? With our biggest intake of interns, was the Lord telling us discipleship was the way forward? The clock was ticking.

There is a time for everything.
Ecclesiastes 3:1 NIV

'Who Am I?'

Like a flood victim clinging onto a log in a torrential river, I clung to this verse from Isaiah at the end of 1994.

Let the one who walks in the dark, who has no light,
trust in the name of the LORD and rely on their God.
Isaiah 50:10b NIV

A decision needed to be made about a geographical location and what the heart of YD would look like. I knew what I was dreaming for YD's future, but where and how was beyond me.

As a baby grows in a womb, the passion to have a Discipleship Training

Centre (DTC) was growing in my heart. It had been in embryo form for years but by the end of this year, I journalled, 'I finish the year convinced a DTC is meant to happen.'

The DTC concept had lain dormant in my heart from my later days in OAC (the late 70s). Now, the bear had awoken from its ten-year hibernation. I dreamed of a school building where young people could have hands-on discipleship. The other problem was, the fire in my belly to see schools reached with the gospel burnt as fiercely as ever. Was I schizophrenic? Did I need to make a choice between raw evangelism or discipleship? Or could they co-exist?

We had looked at Norwood Primary as a possible new YD location. It looked fabulous. But the government wanted two million dollars for it, plus we would need to go into development mode, subdividing the land into lots and selling them to cover costs. I felt like a little boy, living in hope that his mum would buy him the biggest lolly in the shop when she only had five cents.

I drove out and looked at a primary school at the back of Eltham. Hmmm … it just didn't feel right. We had also considered other primary schools as possible locations. We had no idea where we would get the cash to finance such a wild dream.

The mere fact I was looking at schools with excitement and available office space betrayed where I stood on the issue of vision.

I had been praying all year for a miracle (in terms of a million dollars) and nothing happened. I thought, 'What a great story for a book. We trusted the Lord, a million came in and great was the rejoicing.' But nothing came. I clung to my verse about walking in the darkness. The darkness was an all-consuming uncertainty. The pressure was immense.

Circumstances gave us no divine direction. Yes, we had our biggest intake of interns. But we were also deep in the outreach work: in forty schools in Melbourne, three in Tassie, eight in South Australia, eight in Western Australia, eight in New South Wales, with potential for four in Townsville and four on the Gold Coast. By the end of the year we were in over eighty schools, and Lindsay was saying, 'I could go to Queensland and set up a branch.'

Meanwhile we wrestled, like a fourteen-year-old trying to find their identity, with what YD was to become.

Have you ever been stumbling in the dark like this? Hold on with Isaiah 50:10. Even though it is so hard when the pressure is on, trust and rely on the Lord.

Dropping the Orange!

My Dad used to pick up an orange out of the fruit bowl and throw it in the air. He'd pick up another and another until he was juggling four. I used to stare and wonder, 'How does he do that?'

When I practised in secret, I was hopeless. I could play most sports to above-average proficiency, but juggle? Not so much. I was very uncoordinated.

I have little sympathy for people who pick up too many balls in their life and head towards burn-out. Yet in 1995, I found myself in that very predicament, juggling too many activities. How did it get like this? Two reasons. The first was that some of the balls were relational stressors, not activities. The second was that the Lord kept throwing new balls in. Or so I perceived it.

Excuse me mixing up balls and oranges, but have you ever felt you are dropping the oranges, or that the Lord is throwing you a new orange when you aren't expecting it? The stress levels climb, don't they?

Here are the oranges I was trying to juggle during 1995. I felt oranges coming from everywhere.

First, at the start of the year we had no office – and nowhere to go.

Second, I had eight interns plus staff to house by the first of February.

Third, our first family wedding was rushing towards us. Kim was marrying Michael. Have you experienced a first family wedding? Do you remember the pressure?

Fourth, our schools work was taking off. In 1980 I had prayed that we would be in a hundred schools by 1996. We were almost there a full a year early: by the end of 1995 we were in ninety-nine schools.

Fifth, our interstate schools went into overdrive. We were in forty-eight schools in Victoria, sixteen in Queensland, fifteen in South Australia, ten in Western Australia, six in Tasmania and four in New South Wales. We were trying desperately to serve each church in these states, but with limited staff. Lindsay Tunbridge, who was in charge of interstate schools, had a massive job with all the oranges he was juggling.

Sixth, our son, Jamie, was sorting out where his faith was, while our youngest, Nicole, was studying for VCE. Suffice to say, this all led to interesting family discussions!.

Seventh, Pam and I were trying to come to grips with letting Kim go. I remember it hitting Pam the morning after the wedding. We were glad for Kim and Michael, but we felt a real emptiness.

Eighth, the staff and the board remained split on the YD identity issue.

Ninth, a lump in Pam's thyroid threatened to be cancerous.

Tenth, with eight interns and a young staff, the amount of counselling for the baggage they carried was enormous. I hadn't yet learned to delegate.

Eleventh, Lindsay told me at the end of the year he was leaving. This was the first of many times I felt gutted by the loss of staff because I had lost a friend.

And I can't believe I wrote this next statement in mid-1995: 'If there was a soft option, I'd take it.'

I was juggling enough oranges to keep a juice factory going! Was this the cost?

I was struggling to hang on. Fortunately, the Lord persevered with me.

Keep me safe, O God, for in you I take refuge.
Psalm 16:1NIV

Friends

Dear Dad,

Hi! I'm sitting in Australian studies bored to tears, while Mr Woithe has an argument with Malcolm that started when we first walked in. Firstly, Dad I thought you were fantastic on the weekend and I was in absolute awe when those two hundred and thirty-six people stood up on Saturday night and although you thought you were hopeless on Sunday night at Mitcham, you were in my opinion absolutely RADIANT.

Nicole

All our kids have backed us to the death over the years. They have written letters like this one, affirmed me and listened to countless 'Dad sermons'. Many times, after preaching, I've wrestled with darkness – no matter how many responded. These dear kids of ours have been more than kids. They've been friends.

Alongside family, the Lord washed up on the shore of our lives some incredible friends at different times. As time went by, the tide carried them away and new friends arrived.

During the years 1994 to 1996, the Lord provided some key people in my life to sustain me as I walked on squashed oranges!

Phil Burns had a building project company, which managed the building of hospitals and other facilities, both overseas and in Australia. He was a gun at the big picture stuff. He was a very warm and engaging friend.

Warren Sierak, who owned a small electronics business, had (in contrast to Phil) an eye for detail. Best of all, he listened well. Another good friend.

Meanwhile, I had built a network of people in Perth. I felt incredible warmth and welcome from Bruce Eagles and his family (a pastor for Warwick Church of Christ). Then there were Ric and Ais Maxwell, who gave me countless days of free board, and Lyn Devlin, who worked with Youth Vision, the youth department of the Church of Christ. They all became great friends.

All these friends contributed, in significant ways, towards this pivotal time in YD. They never met each other and were all very different. The common denominator was the friendship they offered me during a time when I was struggling.

If it's true that I felt the Lord was throwing me too many oranges, it's also true that he threw me many friends. I didn't look for them; God just provided them. Just as the Lord provided finance for us to survive, so he provided friends for the same reason.

Thank the Lord for the friends you have. Isn't it true that they have held you up when you were buckled at the knees?

**Many will say they are loyal friends, but who
can find a friend who is really faithful?**
Proverbs 20:6 (NLT)

When God Is Silent but Still Speaks

Here I am with over seventy years on the clock, yet I still have moments when I struggle to pick up the Lord's cues on what he is trying to say to me.

Here's something that sounds totally contradictory but is profoundly true: there are times when God is silent but still speaks. He plays a melody in the background that is so easily missed. As I reflect on perhaps the most significant event in YD's history – finding the right premises – I hear a divine melody coming through the events that led up to it.

On January 25, 1995, I wrote to our YD supporters listing three options for an office. There was the option of renting Plenty Primary School, which had been bought privately, for $350 a week. There was a factory in Heatherdale for rent at $150 a week (but as bare as a baby's bottom). Then there was some office space in Box Hill – but it turned out to have prohibitive rent.

All three fell through. Complete duds.

The Lord was saying nothing. I had my ear to the ground waiting. Nothing. Nothing through the Scriptures or a Holy Spirit conviction or a godly Christian's perception or unique circumstances – all the ways I usually discern the Lord speaking to me. Nothing. How do you handle that?

We had only two criteria for YD's accommodation: one, something financially viable to rent and two, a conviction that 'this is the locality the Lord wants us to set up base.'

But still, nothing was happening. On February 2, I wrote in my journal, 'Lord, I just feel out of it. My head has been aching heaps … you know, Lord, I only want your will. Your will be done.'

That month, the verse on the top of our YD prayer letter, named *Prevailer*, was this: 'We do not know what to do, but our eyes are on you' (2 Chron 20:12 NIV).

My first sporting passion, since I was a teenager, was tennis. When Wimbledon came around, I would be out on the local courts playing my heart out. I was playing night tennis and getting to know a number of guys from the area. One of those was a fellow named Alan Dixon, a local estate agent. He put in an offer on a shopfront for us in Panfield Avenue, North Ringwood, with garage space at the back. It would cost us $750 a month for twelve months. We got it.

We took it and moved in, grateful for the provision. And yet, the second criterion wasn't fulfilled in my heart. Was this really the place the Lord wants us to permanently set up base? The shopfront offered us office space and garage space, but it didn't really feel like home. The walls out the back had mould growing out of them. What's more, it was an icebox! We tried using a kerosene heater, and everyone had ash coming out of their noses.

Yes, it was a provision – but we did not feel that the issue of a home for YD was settled. We pressed on, seeking the Lord for a location. Still there was silence, but the melody of circumstance was playing.

What do you do when the Lord is silent? Was he working on something bigger, or was soot in our nostrils his final answer? What would the divine melody reveal?

See, I am sending an angel ahead of you to guard you along the way and to bring you to the place I have prepared.
Exodus 23:20 NIV

The Melody Continues

How do you handle suspense in movies? Personally, I am such a wimp. If it's showing on TV, I lamely excuse myself ('I'm going to the loo!') when things get too tense. If I'm by myself watching a DVD or something pre-recorded, I fast forward the suspense. You always know something is going to happen by the music. There is music for 'the kiss is coming.' There is a different type of music for 'the bad guy is in the cupboard about to ambush the good guy' or again for 'this guy is going to die.'

There was a divine melody playing and the tension was building, but we weren't sure for what outcome. We just knew something was going to happen!

The Lord's melody without words was telling us to keep pressing on for a DTC. Something was going to happen. God's melody came through events and people.

My new friend, Phil Burns, kept the dream alive by continuing to look for a DTC location. I look back now and see that the Lord was using Phil.

In June, we decided to ask the supporters on our prayer list (around seven hundred) what they thought of setting up a DTC. One hundred responded saying 'Yes', with very little negative response. The melody continued.

There were other signs of support. One of our supporters sold a top breeding bull and gave the money towards the DTC. An elderly lady, Miss Lethbridge from Warracknabeal, gave us a thousand dollars for the DTC.

Then one of our schools workers, Jenny McSolvin, rang on July 17 to tell us of an experience she'd had. She had read a passage in Nehemiah about the need for someone to lead the way. She thought it was for her but had drawn a blank. When she read my letter to supporters about the DTC and how I had referred to Nehemiah, she was overjoyed and told me emphatically that this was the way to go.

The melody kept playing.

Jeff Kennett, the Victorian Premier, was still selling off schools, and we'd looked at Norwood Primary School, but two million dollars seemed a bridge too far...

Then in July one of Pam's friends, Erica Tracy, told Pam that Warrandyte South Primary School was possibly going for sale. Erica's children went there; my brothers had gone there also. It caught my attention. Was this the place the Lord wanted for us?

Only one intern had at that stage applied for internship in 1996. Were we to purchase a school for discipleship with just one student, Owen Prout, on our books?

What is that melody you play, Lord?

In August, I wrote in my diary, 'DTC is dead in the water!' I was clearly still not feeling convinced. Was I being like a 'double-minded man ... unstable in all they do' (James 1:8 KJV) or was I like the father who said to Jesus, 'I believe. Help thou my unbelief!' (Mark 9:24 KJV)?

The board was great during this time, providing objective feedback on the whole DTC concept. They still weren't unanimous about the concept. This was not a bad thing.

Finally, we decided to do an assessment on the South Warrandyte School and put in a fee application. My friend Warren paid for this. My diary reveals how uncertain I remained as I wrote 'Lord, this is going to take a miracle to happen.'

On March 7, 1996, a delightfully gracious man by the name of Ron Nethercott said Mission Enterprises would lend us $350,000. Ron had heard me preach at his church the year before and showed a lot of interest in YD from this time onwards. The melody was playing more strongly now.

On March 9, the board said, 'Go ahead'. Everyone on the board was on board!

We had no money; the insides of our empty pockets were flapping in the wind. So we sent a letter to our supporters telling them we were putting in a tender on South Warrandyte Primary School and were seeking pledges towards its purchase. By the end of the month, we had over $100,000 pledged. Then two other organisations that had the same heart as YD indicated that they were keen to move in with us and rent if we were successful in our application.

Our tender figure was $325,500 and we were still $225,000 short in pledges. Yes, we had the money to borrow from Mission Enterprises, but on our present income I didn't know how we could keep up with the repayments. Nonetheless, the board said 'Go'. It was a step of faith for provision.

There was one last hurdle. Would the council let us have a permit to continue as an educational facility at South Warrandyte? We waited and waited on an answer. Then Andrew McCulloch, a Christian guy working for the council, was about to move to another council when he heard of our plight, so he made sure it got through – the week he left.

South Warrandyte Primary School became ours in early 1996. It needed some work. If my memory serves me right, we took out over three thousand staples from the school walls. We painted till we never wanted to see a paintbrush again. I'll be forever grateful to the staff and students who were slave labour through the months of May to July that year.

Buildings aside, it was beautiful. Imagine a bush setting with tall gums, no noise but the sound of nature and a glorious sunset as you walk out the door to go home. I have never worked in a more tranquil setting. The almost five acres of land is gentle and undulating. It is a superb property.

Sometimes God speaks in an unmistakeable way to us. It may be through Scripture, a remarkable circumstance that has divine fingerprints all over it, a supernatural event, a conviction … whatever it is for you, you know 'This is God speaking.'

The purchase of the property had no such feel about it. There was just a series of minor events, nothing spectacular. Yet the sum of all of these gave us a sense there was a divine melody playing in the background. We just knew God was in this.

Living on the Edge

Living on the edge. What does that mean?

How difficult it is to trust the Lord when you know that if he doesn't deliver you will disappear like rain down a drainpipe. I'm sure you've been in this kind of situation: 'If I tithe this money, I won't have enough to pay the mortgage.' In this instance, to tithe is to trust in obedience, but the potential consequence is to disappear down that financial drainpipe.

In 1996, when we had purchased our South Warrandyte property, we were really living on the edge financially. Faith and fear were in hand-to-hand combat. After the euphoria of moving into our new property, we faced some enormous financial battles. Countless times we thought, 'If the Lord doesn't come through, we are headed for ministry oblivion.'

On top of this, we were dependent on the pledges promised for the building. Over a third who promised never delivered. As an organisation, we had taken a huge step of faith. To an outsider, it would have looked like we were living one step from extinction.

Yet the Lord saved us again and again.

Here's an example of the Lord's frequent provision. We needed $1,680 in November 1996. A total of $1,640 came in the mail – and one day before the deadline, Mandy, a staff member, remembered she had a gift of $50 on her. Wow! $10 over!

The Lord of 1996 for YD is the same Lord of today. He is your Lord and mine. Don't let fear conquer and walk out of the ring a victor.

It is I; do not be afraid.

John 6:20b NIV

Sunburn

I've never seen a suntanned iceberg. And for the same reason, you'll never see me looking bronzed after a day at the beach. The iceberg and Rob don't tan!

Any pale, lily-white-skinned person will identify with me. You know how it goes. You didn't realise you forgot your sunscreen until it was too late, and wake up the morning after a day at the beach looking like a gleaming red stop light on a moonless night! Or perhaps you missed covering an arm with lotion, leaving you with one scorched limb that resembles a freshly boiled lobster.

From 1997 on, YD started to change, but like the morning after sunburn we didn't realise it until after the event. Chris Danes moved from Templestowe Baptist to YD staff. He set up a Senior Schools Program for YD. It was very different to what we had been doing. Our style had been proclamational, but Chris' programs for senior students were relational, building relationship with Year 11 and 12 students through coffee and card games and then sharing the gospel personally as the opportunity arose. This changed the look of our schools work. A church could now run two lunchtime programs a week in the one school: the sharing of the gospel by upfront devotions for juniors and the sharing of the gospel through personal friendship with seniors.

Chris drove this program like a red Ferrari at a Melbourne Grand Prix. It took off!

In the years prior to this one, a YD staff person had usually done a bit of everything. Now, staff began to focus on a particular role. This concept of specialising grew; a staff person might specialise in teaching our interns, or be in senior programs or in junior programs in schools. Diversity of jobs in YD meant more opportunity for different gifts, which meant that a broader spectrum of people could work with us. What's more, our internship program began to offer a second year, which in turn increased the need for teachers and disciplers.

We also started to gain some big personality types among the male staff. They were the kind of guys you could hear coming from miles away. These larger-than-life staff were Raff Agostino, Chris Danes, Owen Prout, Steve Peach, Dan Lian and, later, Arty Fiedler. Putting them together on YD staff was like dropping a cigarette butt into a fireworks display box at New Year. All were incredibly full of energy and noise. Wow, did the fun and noise levels in YD town go up tenfold that year.

Have you had change sneak up on you and only realised the impact later? Perhaps all your kids have left home. Or your church has turned over a completely new pastoral team in two years. Or you've just married, changed jobs and moved to a new suburb. How about the move from two children to three children, which has turned out to be a bigger impact than expected?

Sometimes change can be like sunburn. You didn't see it coming until it starts to hurt you.

I learned God can change things awfully quickly if he wants to. The sunburn for me was knowing how to lead these highly talented but forceful guys.

I was about to get lesson 101 in leadership.

Going Under

Some of you will remember Cathy Freeman winning the 400 metres at the Sydney Olympics in 2000? It was like the earth stood still in Australia. It felt almost as astounding as humankind taking that first step on the moon!

How about January 1, 2000? Again some of you will remember, there was that huge 'Y2K' scare. The computers of the world were going to melt down because they weren't configured to cope with the turn of a new millennium.

The year 2000. It was a year that stretched the elastic band of my call to its breaking point. I still have trouble discerning what was the devil, what was trial from the hand of God and what was my own sinfulness or lack of gifting in leadership. It is very easy to make judgments – and, incidentally, dangerous to do so when one is not alert to all the facts. Even what I relate now will have holes in it.

I have always viewed the community of YD as a railway station, where the Lord brings his children, with their baggage, for different periods of time. Our prayer is that, when a person leaves, that precious child of God will have left some of that baggage behind and be closer to Jesus.

In this period in the life of YD, we had many within the community, staff and student population who had loads of personal problems – possibly more that we could handle. There were all sorts of issues. Rocky marriages, incredible anger rooted in past history, fragile connection to local church, anxiety attacks, depression, grief over the death of loved ones, staff feeling disconnected from each other, staff struggling to accept each other.

When you work on building community, the baggage not only comes out, but the bags are ripped open and contents are dumped on the ground.

The luggage sitting on the platform at the YD railway station caused wave after wave of complaint about YD and my leadership. Two staff told me I was the cause of their problems. They were possibly right! Some of the complaining was unfair and some on the mark.

In the midst of this, Pam and I were wrestling with losing all our kids from the family nest. We missed them terribly. I started feeling my age and praying for a successor. Yet I wrote in my journal, 'Give me till I am at least 65 at YD.' It shows where my head was at – I wanted to resign yet stay!

On the June Queen's Birthday weekend that year, my face went numb, my stomach became nauseated and a migraine took over. I slept most of the weekend. My body was screaming at me, 'Enough!' Several people – a lady at our mixed netball competition and a local café owner – commented within a short space of time on how awful I looked. When strangers start telling you that you look like refuse in a garbage bin, you start to take notice.

To top it off, Jamie, our son, was getting married to his fiancée in two weeks' time, and I was to conduct their marriage. Stress and sadness were weighing me down. A diary entry in July reads, 'I just feel sad inside.'

No doubt you, too, have had times where you've felt life being choked out of you, times where you have moved beyond who is at fault to simply recognising that you're going under.

Why, my soul, are you downcast? Why so disturbed within me? NIV
Psalm 42:11a

The Lord gave me some significant friends during this period of my life. One of these was Bob Salamons. He worked tirelessly on our YD property, and in the process became a great friend outside of my YD community of staff and students. He gave ear to my heart's cries and dreams. He's a friend to this very day.

A Dagger

It's my job to put the wheelie bins out. Normally it's a quiet walk in the crisp air of an evening. It was bin night, April 17, 2001. My wiring is not overly bent towards the mystical, so an intuitive God moment, as I rolled out the garbage bin, was not on my agenda.

As I gripped the bin that night, however, a thought gripped my heart: 'There is something else in store.' Was it a storm or a brilliant spring morning? I had no idea. Time was to reveal that this 'something else' was a storm, and great would be the turbulence for YD and me!

This storm was a collection of tough circumstances.

There were so many blockages to our ministry. Something needed to be moved.

By 2001, we had around thirteen on staff. But at a staff retreat in September of that year, all but two had confessed to wanting to quit during the previous twelve months. Several admitted they wanted to leave and do it by themselves, due to frustration with me. My leadership appeared to have more holes in it than a block of Swiss cheese.

Meanwhile, my two key lieutenants, whom I loved so much, were going into meltdown over personal issues.

In 2000, I'd had a lump on my neck. I'd gone in to have it operated on, only to be told by the surgeon that it had disappeared. It was a miracle! Great rejoicing followed. But eleven months later, on March 2001, it returned – and all the fears that came with it.

We owed $17,000 in superannuation to staff. For an organisation dependent on gifts, this was like a mountain sitting on my chest. How could we pay it?

But the knockout punch came in the form of a meeting that I will never forget.

Some leaders from one local church, who had commissioned one of my staff, were less than happy with how we were handling this staff member. They had many valid points, but then it became personal. One church leader turned to me in the presence of everyone else – including the staff person and the chairperson of our board – and told me I was washed up, I was way past my use-by date. Too old!

How powerful is the tongue? Words can pierce your very being like a dagger. Over a dozen years have passed since that day, and now, of course, it is water under the bridge. But at the time, it cut deeply. Do you know that feeling when something someone says stays echoing in your ears and everything else becomes static? This was my experience.

The storm had come. It was a howling gale. And YD and me were right in its path.

Death and life are in the power of the tongue. ESV

Proverbs 18:21

Fish Can Still Be Caught In the Storm

Given that I'm an uncoordinated fisherman who couldn't catch a fish in a tin of sardines, it might seem ludicrous for me to make a pronouncement about fishing. Yet here I go: fish are harder to catch in a storm when your boat is sinking.

In YD's stormy tumult of 2000 and 2001, we still caught fish.

Five years earlier, I had dared to dream that we could have an active weekly Christian witness in over one hundred schools. In 2000, we hit the hundred mark. This was remarkable. Not only had I dreamed of something that seemed impossible, but I'd also dreamed some more for the ultimate demonstration that it was of God. And it became clear to me that it was. We had a lot of fishing lines in the water during the internal storm at YD. This had to be God at work, because we were catching fish while we felt the boat was sinking.

We had schools in country Victoria, capably looked after by Jim Stevens. We had fifteen schools in Perth, overseen by Lyn Devlin. There were four schools in Brisbane and three on the Gold Coast. Mike Gagg, Luke Willey and Donna Savill were about to grow this to an even larger number. The Lord had provided us with Peachy (Steve Peach). Apart from being a fellow Bombers supporter, he was an outstanding all-rounder with numerous giftings, but his greatest contribution was to develop and grow our interstate schools work.

There were more lines in the water as the storm raged on. Arty Fiedler came onto staff to work with Chris Danes in mid-2001. These two capable guys took the concept of reaching senior secondary students in schools to another level. Towards the end of 2001, we were running over twenty of these programs in schools.

And how great is it when the Lord provides voluntary workers who are as devoted to your vision as those who are paid to do the same? Alan Oldman came and gave a regular day a week to do what I saw as the administratively boring tasks. He worked on our finances and later on our schools materials – and in a freezing shed, at the back of our property, no less. Bob Jarrott did the same as a board member, wading through pages of a staff policy manual.

God does provide, not only materially but humanly. The Bible is full of people who get a one-time mention: a builder, a garment maker, a head of a family, a servant. We would never have seen as many lines in the water if we staff had not been released for our tasks by our devoted voluntary workers.

Don't ever forget to say thank you to those who are doing the unpaid work for you. Their hearts cannot be questioned, because there is no material gain from their contribution. What's more, such service allows others to put more lines in the water.

The storm was beginning to recede.

He got up, rebuked the wind and said to the waves, 'Quiet! Be still!' Then the wind died down and it was completely calm.

Mark 4:39 NIV

A Duck's Mind

I sat about thirty metres above the Yarra in South Warrandyte. I was alone, perched on a cliff edge, gazing down on the rippling water of our famous muddy Victorian river, the Yarra. Every Monday morning, for this season of my ministry, I would go and reflect on the past week and plan for the future week at this little haven. It was my attempt to be still in my heart during stormy times in ministry.

One particular day, I'm gazing down at the Yarra River gurgling below me and I see these ducks calmly paddling around in the glistening, sun-struck river. And I felt a longing well up in me: 'O, for a duck's mind!' How great it would be to be puddling in tranquil water with not one anxious arrow imbedded in my mind.

Stillness is so important in stressful times. I was to learn this again at the end of my ministry in YD.

The Lord gradually started to restore normalcy to our community. In April 2001, I wrote in our newsletter, 'Do you know when you feel the wind turning around so it is at your back?' I later journalled, 'I am encouraged by numerous words and actions over the last month … the staff are starting to pray together.'

My stillness before the Lord and the staff's desire to pray together started to still the violence of the storm we had experienced.

Can we ever really grasp how powerful is the seeking heart of God's people? 'Seek and you will find' (Luke 11:9c NIV). But you will find this seeking difficult if you don't learn to be still first.

The Lord started to give us encouragements in ministry. Look at what the Lord did at this camp. It was a sign of the stillness the Lord was restoring.

> Dear Rob,
>
> I just wanted to write to thank you for coming to speak and to encourage you that you were truly used by God on that night. For the past week or so, I have constantly been hearing 'When Rob said this', or, 'That message about our tool boxes really spoke to me', by so many people at my church. There were people crying, repenting and opening their hearts throughout the building that night, and since then I have seen a rape victim release her anger and hurt and a searcher accept Jesus into her heart as a result of what God said through you.
>
> Thank you for your openness in being used by him and keep up the great work.

Isn't the Lord good! It was like he was gently bending down and tending the wound inflicted months earlier in that statement about me being 'washed up'. My own storm was dissipating.

A Pseudo-Ultimatum

I love balconies in auditoriums. They bring grandeur to the building. I remember preaching in the Baptist Tabernacle in Tasmania, with its magnificent balcony. It was an awesome experience.

Our 2001 Summer Outreach commissioning service was held in the Luther College auditorium in Croydon, Victoria. It had a balcony. In those days we filled the Luther Chapel, including the balcony. We were surrounded by music and worship, and there was an amazing vibe. You know when you ask yourself the question, 'Will heaven be like this?' It felt like that. Best of all, we saw God touch people's lives. An intern's mother came to the Lord that night.

A little girl came up to me after the service and said, 'I have seen the face of Jesus for the first time.' My heart just melted. God was so, so good to us in these yearly special services. Astoundingly, many of these services across the years went for up to two-and-a-half hours in sweltering summer heat, with no air conditioning. Yet the Lord moved beyond physical hindrance to bless us.

Yet by January 2002, I needed the eyes of that little girl to see the face of Jesus again. The personal issues of staff, including my own, were returning and gradually overpowering us. What do you do when the personal problems in the lives around you feel suffocating, even as you are trying to deal with your own stuff?

It was becoming clear that our vision to reach students in schools had an anchor holding it back. And that anchor was us! I had difficult questions to ponder. Should I dump those I believed in (with deep personal issues) so the vision could be fulfilled? Or was there a bigger picture behind it all?

The Lord and I had a meeting. I tried to give an ultimatum to Jesus. I told the Lord on January 10, 2002, 'If this year doesn't bring significant change in staff relations, I need to step aside as director.' My leadership felt bankrupt.

It's difficult to explain the feeling of failing in leadership. It eats at the core of your being. When you are male, it is so easy to find your significance in what you do, rather than who you are in Jesus. Looking back, I can see that I fell for this trap. This kind of thinking becomes the Achilles' heel of your self-esteem. I felt I couldn't walk this path any more.

Nonetheless, we battled on as staff and got through this time. During the next few years, I received some lovely encouraging and affirming notes that enabled me to keep trusting the Lord in my inadequacy.

In 2004, one of my staff wrote these words to me:

> Your biggest mistake has been believing in people when no one else would have. [Five staff names, including the author's, were then listed.] How many chances do these people deserve? How long does the big vision have to be put on hold while you nurse us 'cot cases' through? I have seen you do it with others, and I have experienced it myself. I shouldn't be here. You believed in me when I wanted to walk away from everything … you have personally taken on rubbish and never stopped giving us chances.

There is an incredible joy when a family works out their stuff together. But how does it happen?

Remember the little girl who said, 'I have seen the face of Jesus for the first time?'

That's how! Start looking at Jesus instead of the issue. Let your mind stare at him, not the problem. Gaze on him. It may be the first time or the thirty-first time, but keep gazing 'until the things of earth grow strangely dim in light of His wonder and grace.'

Family

I can't play the kazoo or the paper and comb, but for some weird reason I have always liked the trombone. Jamie (our son) told me the other day that I made him play the trombone when he was in Year 7. Of course, we nagged Jamie to practice, but he informed me just last week that he hated it. The 'umpa' of the trombone just didn't grab him. Nonetheless, in his early years at secondary school an inferno of passion for music was set alight that has never gone out.

In 2000 and 2001, Jamie had sailed through two years of internship at YD, a huge step in itself for him. Internship provided an opportunity for the student and the staff of YD to take a good look at each other. It enabled both parties to assess whether they felt YD to be a good ministry fit for the intern. After his internship, Jamie applied successfully for a YD staff position.

I look back with warmth and deep appreciation at the period of time Jamie and I had working together. It was a significant time of ministry. We are both wired as evangelists, so to work together to reach young people in schools was a good match.

The first meeting we did together was with a couple of our interns at a morning seminar at Flinders College. Nothing extraordinary happened. However, I was so aware as we drove to Flinders, took the program and drove home, that my son was with me. I think I was soaking in the wonder and privilege of my son knowing Jesus and talking to others about it. I had an awareness that God had done a work in Jamie's life, and I was enjoying it. There were to be many more times where we shared the gospel together.

Jamie started at the end of November 2002. The board asked some hard questions before he started. 'Will Jamie's love of music compete with YD's passion to share the gospel with youth?' They were both strong loves in Jamie's life. Could they be married together?

A short time after Jamie started at YD, I remember us walking along a worn river track beside the Yarra in Warrandyte. It was a special and significant time as we dreamed together about using multimedia and music for outreach in schools. As we talked, we found a way that would enable Jamie's two passions to complement, rather than compete with, each other. It was to be a hard road, but we would make it.

Another question from the YD board had been about how we, as family members, would function together as co-workers.

Kim, our oldest daughter, had already been on admin staff before Jamie rocked in. She had used her creative and administrative gifts to rescue YD when we were going through an incredible period of growth in schools. Again, I had bathed in God's goodness and blessing of working with our own child. But the issue of a work–family tension had not been raised with Kim. She had just finished university, and it looked as if her time with us would be temporary; I was just giving her some work to keep her out of trouble and help YD out. (As I write now, Kim remains involved in YD, lecturing and counselling staff and students!) Kim gradually 'slid' into the YD family, whereas Jamie's arrival was more sudden and unexpected.

But wait – there's more. Michael, Kim's husband, came onto the board around the same time as Jamie came on staff. I had grown to love and appreciate this young man and his heart for the Lord. I felt I could submit my heart to him as a board member.

To tangle the web even further, Jamie was married to Janie, who had been an intern at YD in 1999. (Janie was to go on to work in our local church for a period of time.)

So, all in all, I had family involved at a number of levels in the ministry. (We haven't even started to talk about Pam and YD. That is another story!)

Was it easy for us to have family in YD? How did the staff and students cope with the boss' family being part of the YD community? How does one avoid nepotism in a scene like this?

As an unbiased dad (fat chance of that!) I saw that my family members had exceptional gifts and great hearts for Jesus. I loved having them around and having the privilege of working with them. Yet, I didn't trust my judgement when it came to putting family on staff. There were times when they were on staff when I didn't trust my judgement with regards to major decisions involving them. How do you get around this?

The answer we came up with was to give that decision to someone else. That someone else was the YD board. I have always believed in accountability, and I had such a good relationship with the board that I knew they would not hold back if I made any decision that smelled of nepotism.

I can't speak completely for the staff and their reaction. I guess it's a bit hard for them to jump up and down and cry 'Favouritism'! For this reason, as with all staff, I deferred to our executive on major decisions involving family.

The hardest issue was probably the one faced by my kids. They had to deal with decisions I made at YD that they found unpalatable. I was their boss at work yet their dad at home. How do you handle that? With difficulty.

It did bring moments of strain on us as family. Ask Pam and the kids! On reflection, though, I feel the benefits far outweighed the negatives. It can work with the right folk in control. When you have a board that cares for all concerned, is prepared to make a hard decision and has the final say, it works.

Too Much Meringue!

If you place in front of me a crispy meringue filled with freshly whipped cream, plump juicy raspberries sitting on top winking at me, I will salivate like a starved Labrador! As a child, I ate a whole bowl of whipped cream and was as sick as the proverbial dog.

If I eat even just one of these drool-worthy meringues, it sets off a voice in my head that says 'more, More, MORE.' If I let my appetite dictate and only ate meringues for meals, the balance in diet would become very obvious in my physique.

My problem in the early 2000s was I was eating too much meringue. I had unknowingly lost balance in ministry.

Across 2003 and 2004, life in the YD office felt rich and fragrant. But as is normal for people, a few staff were struggling. I decided I needed to be as pastorally helpful as possible. It's just something I am wired to do – to try to become 'saviour of everyone', to try to save people in trouble. Oh, but it can be dangerous – a drug, almost. It is so easy to do this in order to feel affirmed and good about yourself rather than to serve. Whatever your gift is, balance is important. Anyone can be guilty of overdosing on their gift to affirm their self-esteem rather than serving God with the right motive.

Part of the YD culture we sought to develop was community, and a huge contributor was our practice of having 'one-to-ones'. Staff members would meet another staff member for about an hour, fortnightly. The students met one-to-one with a staff member, weekly. This practice helped all to feel heard by someone, and it afforded opportunities to minister to one another. It just really worked.

I performed this one-to-one role with senior staff and helped out where a person's regular one-to-one partner was away. I would also catch up with any student or staff member who was having issues their regular partner couldn't handle. On top of this, I was catching up with people in similar roles who weren't part of the YD community. In one week, I recall engaging in eighteen one-to-ones. Some were to mentor, others to debrief, counsel or plan. This was all on top of my normal responsibilities. It was crazy. I had totally lost balance.

Our vision was to reach young people in schools, but I had taken my eyes off the vision. Schools outreach still happened. It was like the sun – it just turned up, every day. But I was caught up in saving the world by counselling everyone on their issues.

At the end of 2003, I wrote, 'I stagger into 2004 totally exhausted.' Like a World War II Japanese kamikaze pilot, who would fill his plane with explosives and dive bomb enemy ships, committing suicide in the process, I was destroying myself by lack of balance in ministry. I had become a kamikaze pastoral worker.

Something interesting resulted at a YD staff level. Everyone was as happy as a carnivore in a butcher's shop. Some were giving themselves to schools work, either junior or senior ministry. Some were giving themselves to teaching. And so it went on, with people working in particular areas. However, when staff were asked to do work outside of their area of expertise and passion, there was a reluctance. It irked me. I look back now and think 'How thick can I be?' I was setting that very example of throwing myself into pastoral work and neglecting the big picture of reaching young people in schools. By example, I was accidentally creating a jig saw puzzle where the pieces didn't want to fit together. I was gorging on the meringue of pastoral care while forgetting to balance my diet with evangelism.

How did the Lord restore balance? I started to take time out each Monday morning to reflect on the past week and the ministry's future. I was desperate to find out why I felt lost. I thought, 'I have to start listening to the Lord.' That's always a good starting point. Gradually, the light went on and I saw what I had been doing. The YD board played a significant part in this discovery.

Next, we had a special staff meeting where I challenged the whole staff about being part of the big picture and not being so obsessed with their own niche. Finally, we restructured YD so that staff not only knew their task but how these fitted into our larger, shared purpose. And I started to get back to my core job, which was to keep the staff aware of our ultimate vision.

Leaders can be selfish in a spiritual way. The ministry I had been doing was spiritual. It was, however, selfish, as I was doing what I liked at the expense of the team. Leaders frequently must sacrifice what they would like to do for the sake of big picture the Lord has laid on their heart.

Paul knew the big picture and would not be distracted from it.

It has always been my ambition to preach the gospel where Christ was not known, so that I would not be building on someone else's foundation …
This is why I have often been hindered from coming to you.

Romans 15:20, 22 NIV

'I've Got Your Back'

What would it be like to have an eye in the back of your head? Pretty handy, I think. In fact, I reckon an ear, as well as an eye, would be helpful. Still, that is not how the Lord has made us.

There have been many faithful servants in the YD office, but the two longest serving have been Linda Schafer and Wendy Waddell. These two names you have more than likely never heard of, but these women gave so much to YD with their incredible faithfulness, and to me they gave something even more powerful. They 'had my back'.

Wendy and Linda had my back in that they were relentlessly faithful to me in work. They were fiercely loyal to YD when dealing with people. They were an invaluable help discerning the spiritual and relational temperature of the YD community. They worked outside of their job descriptions without a word of complaint. They were God's gift to us all.

Wendy started work at YD in 2005, not long after Pam, my wife, started as our finance person. I had been looking for someone to take over as receptionist, Wendy was part of a small group we were in. Peculiar, isn't it, that both Linda and Wendy came to be part of YD as our receptionists via our small groups?

Wendy quickly became a mother figure to our students and to many staff. I don't know how to explain this expression, but the warm greetings to staff, students and visitors were 'mumly'. (Now there's a new word!) This maternal expression went beyond greetings to welcoming warm chats and occasional deeper moments. As I already said about Linda, having this type of person on our front desk really shaped the family feel that developed at YD over the years.

Wendy's creativity was invaluable to me. I could give her an idea I had for a sermon prop and she would deliver, every time. She typed up endless sermons and devotions for me.

I am sure there are many people out there, in ministries far more notable than mine, who would also testify to those who had their back – to the behind-the-scenes person who stuck by them and inadvertently made them look good. Wendy was such a person for me.

I think of Joseph of Arimathea and Nicodemus, two relative unknowns in biblical history. They took the body of Jesus down from the cross. It was an amazing act of service that we now recognise centuries later. They had Jesus' back. We shouldn't neglect or be ungrateful to the people who have blessed us with service in the background.

Taking Risks

There we were, twenty kids on one side of a single bed sheet, another twenty on the other side, and us in the middle holding the sheet up, in a school classroom. The kids couldn't see each other. What's more, they were all totally bored. Why? I had come up with the idea of playing a board game called battleships in our junior high program. It was a spectacular failure. So much so, it became a running joke for quite a few years in YD land.

But we had ideas that floated, too. Secondary school students loved chocolate!

We stumbled on the idea of using chocolate to kick start our new junior schools programs. We used five games involving lots of chocolate to get the students excited about the possibility of coming to our weekly programs. It wasn't all chocolate. We always, on this day, let the students know there would be a weekly 'God talk'. We needed them to understand we were Jesus lovers. It didn't worry them at all.

We encouraged a competitive element to generate excitement. Who could skull a carton of chocolate milk the quickest? Who could catch a chocolate square in their mouth from the greatest height? Or who could feed a blindfolded student a chocolate yogurt container the fastest? The kids loved it.

It was an incredible success when we started it. On one occasion we had between two and three hundred students outside on a bitumen quadrangle, joining in chocolate games at McKinnon Secondary College.

On another occasion, at Maroondah Secondary College, we had no one turn up for our first program. I couldn't understand what was wrong. Then I discovered the church workers involved hadn't put up posters advertising the 'Chocolate Pig Out'. The next week, with posters up, the room was full to overflowing. I clearly remember the chocolate milk skulling race between a Year 7 girl and Year 8 boy. We gave the Year 7 girl a fifteen-second head start over the Year 8. The end result was a promotional dream. The Year 8 boy did not want to be beaten by a girl, so he just poured the milk down his throat until it gushed out of his mouth and all over him. The kids went ballistic. Heaps of them came back the next day to hear the gospel. (I never found out what his mum thought, though!)

This approach would not be considered politically correct these days. How healthy is chocolate? At the time, schools didn't mind what we did (within reason). Of course, it was a risk – we risked complaints from parents or teachers who could potentially close the program down.

But the whole concept of promoting ourselves with chocolate was a smash hit. It overthrew the image of Christians as people incapable of having fun. We did get accused of bribing kids with chocolate, but were never closed down over the chocolate games. While we used chocolate to promote our presence, we wanted no deception. We didn't use chocolate to proselytise students, and we always gave kids the opportunity to walk before we gave a devotion.

Lastly, the big chocolate advertising brought in the rejected, lonely and those labelled 'odd'. We discovered that these students found our weekly programs a haven of safety for one day a week.

Taking a risk may work, or it may blow you away. For some ideas and decisions at YD, we bathed everything in prayer and took careful consideration. With other ideas, we simply pushed against a door to see if it would open. To some, this may sound a little like spiritual Russian roulette, as though we were just spinning the gun chamber and hoping we didn't discharge the solitary bullet when we pulled the trigger. But this wasn't our attitude. We were saying, in effect, 'If this is of you, Lord, put your fingerprints on it. Otherwise, stop it.'

Of course, YD took larger risks than the chocolate games. In wider evangelical circles throughout most of my ministry, the idea of putting on female staff in ministry roles was perceived as a risk: some wouldn't agree theologically with the teaching roles they were given; others felt that stopping to have babies broke staff rhythm; yet others felt it just didn't look right to have an overbalance of women in evangelism. So there were risks to taking on female staff at YD, even though we'd done so since 1987.

Yet in this season the Lord brought a new wave of staff, and many were women. Prior to this, YD had predominantly been populated with big male personalities. Now, it was to flip. The Lord was to raise up some of the finest women I've ever worked with, quiet women who went about their work in a no-nonsense type of way.

There is always someone who will give you a reason not to go ahead with something. Sometimes, their reasoning is sound and needs to be heeded. Many times, however, the main motive for avoiding risk is fear. Personally, I'd rather face that fear and take the risk, trusting the Lord to reveal his will in the process.

Daring decisions often contain risks. Do you take them? I have a rather simple attitude to daring plans. Is it sinful? If not, and if you sense it's the way forward, go for it, knowing our sovereign God loves us and will stop us if we've got it wrong. He knows our heart.

> **You can make many plans, but the Lord's purpose will prevail.**
> Proverbs 19:21 (NLT)

Go to the Hedges

'A snoring bush?' you think to yourself. You push the hedge apart, scratching the palms of your hands in the process. There, lying in a drunken stupor, is a man who has never heard the word 'shave'. His eyes have more red lines than a road map of the USA. He smells. His clothes are filthy and worn. This excuse for humanity looks up at you through bleary eyes and says, 'Huh?' You can't believe what you are about to say. Nevertheless, out come the words, 'Wanna come to my place for a party for a big feed?'

Sound farfetched? It's not, if you have read the story of the banquet in Luke 14 told by Jesus. You know it. A banquet is being held for the neighbourhood, but much to the displeasure of the rich provider the invitations are turned down. He sends his servants to the local streets and alleys and still there are vacant seats at his banquet table. So finally, our provider sends his servants out to find a rent-a-crowd. As the KJV puts it, he sends them to the 'hedges and highways'. This gives the impression the hedges were the furthest extremities from his place.

I sat down with the staff in 2006 and 2007 to share my burden of going to the hedges. It was a case where the evangelist within me took over from common sense.

We were in as many schools as we could get permission to gain entry to;

each schools ministry was owned by a nearby local church. My problem was, there were more schools we could gain entry to, but there were no nearby local churches to own the ministries. The evangelist within me shouted, 'It's not fair that these young people don't hear the gospel just because there is no local church for us to work with.'

The main concern was that there would be no one to follow these kids up. I had no answer to that question. Yet my heart broke for those kids who, in my mind, might as well have been on an island south of the South Pole, they were so without the gospel. Lack of follow-up is not ideal, but neither is hell.

I have been profoundly impacted by the Lord's handling of the man called 'Legion'. After this man's miraculous conversion, Jesus sent him off to a Gentile village with no knowledge of God but for his immediate encounter with Jesus. There was no follow up.

So, we decided we would go to these 'hedge schools' regardless. The staff embraced it. A few years earlier the staff had opposed it; now the winds of change were coming.

God sometimes asks us to do things that seem to defy logic. Is he asking you the same at this moment?

As Jesus was getting into the boat, the man who had been demon-possessed begged to go with him. Jesus did not let him, but said, 'Go home to your own people and tell them how much the Lord has done for you, and how he has had mercy on you'.
Mark 5:18–19 NIV

Significantly, around the same time we made this move to 'hedge schools', the YD outreach band, Selaphonic, was born. Jamie Coyle headed this up. Jamie started going into schools with his band of musicians, using music as a means to start sharing the gospel with secondary-school kids. It was rough and ready at the start, but it worked. We produced a CD with music and a message on it to give away for free to the students – for those who couldn't afford $2!

We were sharpening the pointy end of our ministry, and the whole staff was on board with it. We were going to reach as many students as possible, even if it meant we were going to push a hedge or two back.

A Drought Ends

During the early 2000s, Australia experienced the worst drought I've lived through. It wasn't officially declared as over until 2010.

I've never experienced anything like it. Nature strips were reduced to dirt. Suburban house gardens were wiped out. Water restrictions in Victoria would allow only a couple of hours watering the garden, three times a week. You could only wash your car with a bucket of water. If your neighbours caught you watering on the forbidden days, they could report you. Nurseries only survived by the sudden popularity of cactus plants. There was a surge in the purchase of huge plastic water tanks by suburbanites. Many turned to recycling their greywater. In Toowoomba, Queensland, there was a vote on whether recycled sewerage water would be embraced as a water supply. The vote was defeated. Unbelievably, the inconceivable happened; the Snowy Mountains Hydro Electric station was threatened by lack of water.

Youth Dimension was facing a drought of a different nature. The tried and true methods that had worked in the past were starting to dry up. They were losing effectiveness. We had to do something. On May 19, 2007, we called a Saturday morning meeting of all staff, the board and some specially invited creative thinkers. As I prepared, I remember thinking, 'I have no idea what is going to come out of this.' Ross Grace, one of our board members, was the excellent facilitator for the whole event. He had about as much idea of what would transpire as I did.

At the end of what felt like a Niagara Falls-worth of words being exchanged, one word floated to the surface: 'Internet'.

I walked out excited but dazed. I was not expecting this. What does that mean? Internet? What would ministry look like? I was digitally illiterate.

At the time, Myspace was popular with young people, while the social website, Facebook, was more for the old people of this world! We thought the answer was to set up a website and get young people to hook into it. Who was going to do that? Where were we going to get the money to do it? Were we on the right track? Would this break the drought? Was this what the Lord wanted? How would we know?

We needed cash to set the website up and to do what we dreamed of doing with it. A gift for over $20,000 came in for this purpose. We also needed a person to head it up. Such a person came: Aaron Harvey. This was the beginning of change in YD. While the changes didn't happen overnight, I regard this as a watershed moment in YD story.

Sometimes, you don't realise until much later that an event was a turning point. I drove out that day thinking, 'Oh well, a good talkfest! Internet? That blindsided me. The jury is out; now it's back to a normal Monday.'

Hmmm ... is there ever a normal Monday in Jesus' heart for you?

Plans fail for lack of counsel, but with many advisers they succeed.
Proverbs 15:22 NIV

There had been many advisers. Their counsel was to prove correct.

A Thirtieth Birthday ... but Change Was Coming

Ahhh, nostalgia – the medication of the elderly! Thirty years gone – 1978 to 2008 – with enough stories to make a tapestry of God's goodness to cover the five acres of our YD property.

It was also nostalgic to return in 2008 to my old church to preach. That feeling melted quicker than an ice block on a barbeque. I was greeted by an old friend, whose first question was, 'When are you going to retire?' I had seven others ask me the same question that morning!

At a special YD board meeting in 2008, the talk of succession planning was seriously addressed. There had always been talk over the years about who would follow me, but this time it was starting to sound real. I look back and realise that, as real as those words were, I was computing it at head level but not at heart level. It's like that look you see on a person's face when they receive unbelievably good or bad news: a blank stare. My heart was vacant.

I didn't have a lot of time to think about it, and there were no obvious candidates. There was talk of advertising the position. This made me quiver with repulsion. I really wanted someone homegrown.

At the end of the year, Owen Prout finished up and Jo Bryant left to have her first baby.

Owen had been at YD for thirteen years and was clearly called to move into a local church ministry in Cockatoo. The whole staff, including me, felt his leaving deeply. He had been part of the fabric of YD for so long. He was also the kind of guy everyone liked. He had done much for the vision of YD and had held down a senior position of responsibility. It was a blow to the YD heart.

Jo Bryant's leaving was also tough for us. I had watched this shy young lady blossom through internship, come onto staff and head up our school leavers' discipleship program. Jo had an incredible capacity to complete large amounts of work. Even more importantly, Jo had a teachable heart and a love for Jesus. She had held a key role at YD. Her leaving, as well as Owen's, made us feel we'd been cut off at the kneecaps.

By the way, I do have to confess something here. When our girls on staff announced they were pregnant, I was ecstatic for them as mums-to-be, but I also thought, selfishly, 'How can you leave us? We need you and we'll miss you!'

But as I've had to learn as a leader, there is always a bigger picture for every staff person beyond my own agenda.

Never forget your picture of life is but a microdot in the picture our Lord is creating. I had to remember this through the events of 2008.

Stumbling in the Bush

I've always been an early riser, ever since I was sixteen years old. So, while it might seem like a superhuman effort, especially to those of you who are wired like an owl and come alive at night, rising at 5 am to chat with the Lord was not as heroic as it may sound.

In 2008, I was becoming progressively fatigued. Yet it was not because of early mornings, but rather because of the pressure of ministry. Alongside my leadership role, I was doing heaps of preaching.

I love netball. I have played mixed netball for over twenty-five years and have treasured not only the game but the release it brings to my mind and body. So when I blacked out after a game, Pam said to me, 'You are not resting enough.' However, I knew the solution wasn't more sleep.

In 2008, we refocused our vision in schools. I felt that our new emphasis on outreach through Selaphonic, alongside the development of our multimedia approach through Aaron Harvey, would enable us to eventually reach 4,000 a week in schools. Incredibly, in June of 2008 we had over $90,000 come in to put Aaron Harvey on staff as our media man. It would also buy all the necessary computer equipment we needed. God's people were so good to us.

I had deep feelings about this vision of reaching 4,000 a week. I am not a born crier, yet at a term gathering of all our schools workers, I broke down as I painted the vision of reaching this vision. You know when tears come out of nowhere and just rock into your railway station of public emotion? I felt this call in the core of my heart.

I had an unusual experience in that year. In one of my early morning quiet times, I felt this deep urge to go out to the YD property and walk around it, claiming protection over the ministry. I had done this only once before.

Ever had a moment where you feel the Lord is telling you to do something illogical? This was such a moment! It was 5 am in the morning, pitch black and Melbourne-cold (aka freezing). I was nice and warm, hovering over the heater in our rumpus room reading my Bible, when I felt the pull to go out to the property.

I just had to do it.

So there I was, stumbling round YD in the blackness, which in some areas is thick bush. I thought maybe I could cut corners so I could get home and warm sooner, but no way; the Lord was driving me to pray protection over every inch of that property. This compulsion to pray happened again for another two mornings.

I am not sure where the devil's attack begins and ends on YD in this particular year, but I am sure of this one fact: when you start planning to take down the kingdom of darkness by reaching 4,000 a week in schools, the forces of evil don't like to be poked in the eye.

Years earlier, I had heard of a witches coven that prayed against YD and for the break-up of marriages at a staff level. What do you do with that? Pray.

Youth Dimension was over thirty years old but still of importance to the Lord of the Harvest, enough to get me out of my pyjamas to pray on cold frosty mornings.

The god of this age has blinded the minds of unbelievers, so that they
cannot see the light of the gospel that displays the glory of Christ, who is
the image of God.

2 Corinthians 4:4 NIV

He is patient with you, not wanting anyone to perish,
but everyone to come to repentance.

2 Peter 3:9c NIV

I Should Have Seen It Coming

Just last week I was flying to Queensland with our son, Jamie, back to his home in Coolum. And I thought, 'Here is my opportunity to ask a difficult question.' The time between when he and I had departed YD had put enough water under the bridge to ask this without any angst. What's more, there aren't too many places to escape to on a plane in mid-flight!

At the end of 2009, Jamie and Janie had dropped on us the bombshell that they were leaving for Coolum in Queensland. Jamie asked if YD was interested in setting up a branch there.

Why was this a bombshell? As you would have guessed, we are a tight-knit family, and the thought of anyone moving away from the family den in Melbourne had a heart-wrenching impact on Pam and me.

What's more, from a ministry point of view, it smashed our dreams. We had seen the development of Selaphonic's outreach ministry in schools as pivotal to the 'new' YD. And the digital vision of outreach in schools, which was at the heart of our new endeavours, had been strongly influenced by Jamie. The possibility of losing Jamie therefore tore out our hearts, not only at a family level, but at a ministry level as well.

To cut a long story short, YD didn't think it was ready for a branch in Queensland, yet Jamie and Janie felt called to leave. So leave they did, at the end of 2010.

Have you guessed my question in the plane? You are right: 'Why?'

Ever asked yourself, or someone else, 'Why?' Heart-rending moments do that to you. There are times when the Lord just turns life on its head and sends it in the opposite direction to what you're expecting, leaving you reeling.

Jamie's answer, five years after the event, was interesting. It made me realise that, as a dad, I should have seen it coming.

Jamie drew the analogy of a boy becoming a man and having to move out of home. It was time to 'leave home', ministry wise, and move into his own style of outreach. Interestingly, I had recorded in my diary that he had preached at a nearby local church and four people said after the service, 'You preach like your dad.' Yes, it was the right time for him to move out of the YD environment; there were times when being in Dad's shadow wasn't helpful.

In the last Selaphonic outreach with YD, over a hundred responded, with sixty-three coming to Jesus for the first time. I felt it was like a divine goodbye – a kiss of blessing. It confirmed that it was the right time for Jamie and his family to move on.

As Jamie recounted to me on our plane trip, he had then felt, 'Now I can have my dad back.' The problem was, whenever we were together as a family outside of work, we would talk YD. Ministry had flavoured every area of our lives, to the point that the normal father–son relationship had been strained by ministry.

Isn't it ironic that Jamie leaving to go interstate was to be the means of bringing us closer together? God's ways are certainly mysterious – and always right.

Jamie, Janie and the kidlets stayed with us for a few weeks before they left. It was very special. Pam and I can still remember that empty, hollow feeling as they disappeared up our street to head to their new home in Queensland. Only parents know the deep ache of seeing a son, daughter (-in-law) and grandkids disappear over the horizon.

I should have seen it coming. Emotions, ministry and close relationships certainly can blind one to God's ways.

Sunbaking on a Jindabyne Lawn

Pam and I were reclining in the sun on a delightful, grassy patch of parkland in Jindabyne. Jindabyne is located in the Snowy Mountains just over the Victorian border into New South Wales. We were lazily looking on as the Jindabyne summer outreach team, led by Steve Harris, played games with locals.

My phone rang. It was one of those memory-staining moments. Nicole, our youngest daughter, was screaming frantically down the phone. I couldn't take it in, except that it was clear something awful had happened. I handed the phone to Pam.

Nicole was at a hens' party on one side of Melbourne, with their baby Eli, and had received a phone call from a total stranger saying he had her kids and that Adrian, her husband, was in hospital. He had been innocently riding his BMX with their two kids on the Healesville bike track when he'd had an accident. Nicole thought he might be paralysed.

We felt as if we had been run over by a truck. We were stuck in a motel, over five hundred and eighty kilometres from Melbourne. It was late, so we decided to stay the night and drive back the next day.

That night, we lay in bed wondering if Ade was going to live or die. There was a deep sense of foreboding – cold fear and overpowering numbness. The ongoing phone calls with Nicole did nothing to calm those feelings. It actually fed them. We were to feel this once again, years later.

We learned more. Adrian, Jamison and Jemima had been riding their bikes when Ade had hit a bump and gone over the handlebars, straight onto his head. He'd split his bike helmet down the centre. He would have been in the cemetery if he hadn't had his helmet on.

The next day, we arrived at the Alfred Hospital to see Adrian an absolute mess. The damage to his back was so great, they had had to operate by going in through his chest. They deflated his lungs and moved his heart. The doctors had taken a rib out to help replace a vertebra.

While the doctors were operating, Ade went into heart failure. It was here Ade had the most amazing experience of meeting Jesus. The choice of staying or going to heaven was as clear to him as a billboard sign thirty metres high! Ade felt the Lord prompting him to go back and care for his little family.

Later in that month of January, the doctor told Adrian it was a miracle he didn't become a quadriplegic. He had more metal work in his back than the Sydney Harbour Bridge. For the next few years, Ade was to live on heavy pain-relieving drugs and endure severe physical suffering. For someone who was a man off the land and a landscape gardener, it was very challenging. He was reduced to doing very little physically, as he would face the consequences of greater pain if he tried to extend himself. This was a life-changing moment.

Nicole now had to carry the family, and the grief, while whatever the future had in store for them unfolded. We felt helpless. Do you know that sense of wanting to help, but there is nothing you can do? Don't you hate seeing your children suffer?

Fast forward to the present, and Nicole and Adrian have been all over Melbourne, sharing their story of how the Lord took them through this horrific event. He has healed Ade to such a point that he went back to landscaping and laying concrete – literally a miracle.

The response to their story of God's grace can only be described as remarkable. Scores of folk have responded to their story of pain and healing as it has been shared in all flavours of churches. Now they are leading a church they have planted in Healesville. There's more to their story, but that comes later. But if you, too, are in that place of horror, hope in God.

> **Why are you down in the dumps, dear soul? Why are you crying
> the blues? Fix my eyes on God – soon I'll be praising again.
> He puts a smile on my face. He's my God.**
>
> Psalm 42:11 (*The Message*)

Operations Manager, Where Are You?

Ever had a small cut on your finger and ignored it because you've got so much to do? You couldn't be bothered to find a bandaid; besides, it is only a minor cut. What happens? For the next few days, you are going, 'Yow!' every time you bump it. It's then that you realise why the Lord gave you five fingers instead of four. You need them all.

That's how it felt to me when we lost our operations manager at YD. Steve Harris had been our 'ops manager', freeing me up from the worry about computers, building works, HR and a dozen other things that would otherwise interrupt my day. But by 2009, Steve had moved on and we were minus an ops person. I was going, 'Yow, yow, yow'! I had no bandaid. Steve had left a big hole that I was not coping with, and the cut of need and inconvenience was just not healing.

I was praying like a mantis about it. For a new operations manager to start right away, we needed around $36,000 to cover support for the start of their salary package. This would buy us some time for the new ops person to raise enough regular financial givers to become self-sufficient. In my mind, this was a huge ask. The Lord was going to have to pull someone out of a hat to take on this onerous job.

At the start of 2010, we had to weather Jamie dropping his move to Queensland on us as well as Adrian's life-threatening accident. To add to this, our other son-in-law, Michael, was struggling with his business. Life was interesting, to say the least.

Isn't it fascinating how a crisis drives you to prayer? You may be in one right now.

The Lord had been challenging me about the suffocating effect busyness had on my prayer life. I read a short but convicting quote by one of my old heroes, Robert Murray McCheynne, who said, 'The greatest need of my people is my own personal holiness.' I knew that my walk would not match my work if I didn't spend time with the Lord. McCheynne also says, 'A man is what he is on his knees before God, and nothing more.' Enough said.

All these events drove us to our knees.

We prayed for an operations manager. We prayed for $36,000. We prayed for a sixteen-student intake for that year. We prayed for Michael's job situation. We prayed for Jamie and Janie's future. We prayed for Nicole and Adrian, who were in a world of confusion and pain. We prayed and prayed.

Gradually, over six months, $36,000 came in for the new operations person. Answered prayer.

Sixteen students started at the beginning of 2010. Answered prayer.

However, no one was rushing over the horizon to take on the operations position, and nothing was progressing in Michael's job situation. 'What is going on?' was the silent groan of our hearts.

I journalled this prayer on March 10, 2010: 'Enable Michael to not only find a job but find a future. Lord, encourage him as he and Kim seek your future.' Wow. I had no idea how the Lord was going to answer this.

I had jokingly said to Michael at the end of 2009, 'Want a job doing operations?' We laughed! By July, that laugh had turned into an application from Michael to take the operations position. Remember, Michael was on the YD board and had sat in on numerous discussions over possible candidates for the position. He honestly had no idea the Lord was going to tap him on the shoulder to take this position. When he did apply, the board was tough as they grilled him about his heart and gift suitability for the role. There was an obvious fear of nepotism, and correctly so; but a better move could not have been made.

All of this is testimony to a prayer-answering God. Wouldn't you regard this as miraculous?

Ask and it shall be given.
Matthew 7:7 KJV

… the God who holds in his hand your life and all your ways.
Daniel 5:24b

How true are these promises.

Stinging Eyes and An Uncertain Heart

I'm standing outside in the YD garden on a cool Saturday morning in February 2011, pruning back this peculiar plant with white sap. Two hours later I am in agony, my eyes screaming out in pain. It felt like a blacksmith's red-hot poker has been plunged into them.

The impact on my eyes was extraordinary, the sensation like traffic lights switching from green to red. There would be unbelievable pain for a minute, which would then go away for a minute, only to return. This went on for six hours. It was excruciating.

I got myself to a doctor at a 24-hour medical centre, who gave me some 'fix all' eye drops. They did nothing for a few hours, then the torture finished. To this day, I think the cause was the white sap from those weird plants.

Why was I in the YD garden on a Saturday morning?

The board were once again discussing the future of YD and a possible succession plan. I thought it appropriate that I be absent. It was surreal and unsettling. I always knew this day would eventually come. I remember when our first baby, Kim, arrived, I had the sensation of completely losing touch with what I was feeling – a kind of numbness, like I couldn't feel my own skin. This was my inward reaction to the start of succession planning.

When you have been sitting in the leader's chair for thirty-three years – a chair you actually made, no less – and you are told it's time to get up from that chair, it does tend to unsettle you, no matter how cool a face you put on. Little did I realise that this was to be a three-year season of uncertainty in YD. It was to continue for the whole period leading up to Pam and I leaving.

I have learned one thing about uncertainty. Whether it's uncertainty about health, the kids, your ministry in church, your job, finances or anything else, it's the same scenario: uncertainty spins you out because you lose control. It absolutely stretches trust in Jesus.

Dennis McCurdy, our chairperson, asked for a special meeting with me. I didn't know what it was going to be about, but I felt nervous. The uncertainty factor was dramatically increasing. It turned out the board wanted my input on what I felt the right successor should exhibit in character and gifting. It was very gracious of them to ask for my thoughts.

I shrink and shrivel up inside when I think about my reaction. Anxiety started to build about how Pam and I were going to cope financially. How could I walk down that road of doubt when the Lord had been so faithful in providing for us over a period of forty years in faith ministry? It's amazing how uncertainty and crisis seems to bring about a memory wipe, and you forget what the Lord has done for so many years for you.

Do you ever look at some old saint and think how it must be fantastic to have 'arrived' when you start sprouting grey hairs? I'm no saint, but I do have the grey hairs! The Lord never stops shaping character, and the Lord was taking this sixty-seven-year-old and crunching his character into shape through uncertainty once again. You gotta love that we are children of God and he is forever growing us through the events of life.

Rejoice in your uncertainty. He is merely doing his fatherly thing: growing you!

My son, do not make light of the Lord's discipline, and do lose heart when he rebukes you, because the Lord disciplines the one he loves, and he punishes everyone he accepts as a son.
Hebrews 12:5–6 NIV

Totally!

It must have looked weird: three teenagers carrying on like turkeys on drugs, pretending to drive a car that is sitting on a trailer, being towed to who knows where. On the same trailer is a film crew headed up by Aaron Harvey, filming 'take 76' (a minor exaggeration) on that scene.

During my time at YD, we produced four films which spelled out the gospel as simply as possible. We called them the 'Total Truth' series. The films went for approximately five minutes each. (Check them out on the YD Bulls and Arrows website.) The original purpose was to use them in our summer outreach program. We wanted to be able to have a pointy end to our witness. We didn't want anyone leaving our programs without knowing how a person could come to know Jesus.

Norma was a lady in her seventies who had heard about our summer outreach in Boort, northern Victoria. What a champion she was. She lived in St Arnaud in north-eastern Victoria, about two hundred and fifty kilometres from Melbourne. Norma wanted the youth of St Arnaud, with a population of around two and a half thousand, to hear about Jesus.

Norma called us up and asked us to come, so we sent a team that Christmas to St Arnaud. We didn't know what to expect from this perceived sleepy, needy community.

In second year of summer outreach in St Arnaud, 2012, the team decided to show all four of our Total Truth films on the last night, one after the other. It was like being at an all-you-can-eat restaurant. They got the full four-course dinner of the gospel: God's love, sin's impact, the cross and the need for repentance and faith. It was a plateful of God's truth.

Sitting in the audience was a scruffy older teenager called Robert. It was only his second night. When the films were finished, he turned to a team member, saying that he needed to talk to someone about the films. That night, he stepped into a relationship with Jesus. This was significant, not only for Robert but also for us, as it demonstrated to us that the Lord could use the films we produced.

My goodness, we produced those films so quickly. I drove Aaron and his team mad pushing to get them done before summer outreach happened. We have since showed those films in nearly all our schools. The response has been varied, but at least we can say that we have not held back in pressing people with a sense of urgency to come to know the Jesus.

This was the start of a new direction in ministry – reaching young people through film. Youth Dimension has produced other films since, which we have used extensively to speak to today's youth. Aaron Harvey, Jase Tucker, Dave Powys and Caitlin Salamons contributed a significant amount of time and energy to creatively produce these films. Aaron's ability in this area not only brought a new skillset to YD but also won us recognition from the Christian media. Aaron was God's gift to us in a time when we were wondering, 'Where to next?'

Peculiar as it might sound, this development in film ministry gave me the greatest satisfaction in my sunset years at YD. I must confess, I am a movie fanatic. As I read the Scriptures, I have noticed how the Lord uses the visual to reach his creation. I was reading Psalm 58 this morning and noted how the Lord used eight different pictures to describe the wicked. Then I turned to read some of Revelation, which is likewise saturated with imagery.

The visual is so powerful. Use it to communicate.

Names Named

'Thwak!' or 'Thwonk!'... I'm not sure of the exact sound that David's stone made as it sank into Goliath's head. But how brave was David? Watching this teen stand there with his arm raised, holding up the bloodied, severed head of Goliath, must have been spine-tingling.

Bravery takes all kind of shapes. Standing alone for Jesus in a venomous anti-Christian office takes bravery. Living as a single mum after being deserted takes courage. Telling your boyfriend it's over because you know this guy isn't God's choice takes inestimable fortitude.

It was one of the bravest decisions made by a board member. On November 24, 2012, in a YD board meeting, with the founder (me!) present, names were called for a possible successor. It was a pivotal moment in this next critical step for YD.

For over a year, there had been talk about what YD would look like in the future and what attributes would we look for in a successor. This felt all very safe – until names were named. I felt great respect from the board. I have to take my hat off to our chairperson Dennis McCurdy, and to Ross Grace and Sally Agostino, who helped move the board to this next vital step. In my mind, it took guts.

'Who do you think could be our next CEO?' A question along these lines was asked. There was an awkward silence, and then the names came forward. As they did, I felt my life, and my thirty-six years at the helm, passing before my eyes.

I am not sure why, because I had prayed regularly for a successor throughout the year before this meeting. On a holiday in Palm Cove, Queensland, that February, I had written, 'Lord, I pray for a God-anointed successor. Lord I can't do it, you can.' Later in March, I prayed again, 'I wait for you to send an Elisha.' On June 1, I prayed, 'Thanks, Lord, for a sense you will look after my successor at YD.' And I prayed in September, 'Lord, for the person to succeed me, be preparing them. Encourage them.'

So here I am in November sitting dumbstruck, with the Lord answering my prayers. Names are being considered. Isn't it true sometimes that we can't get a handle on answer to prayer?

The board's concern was not just for my handling of this situation, but for Pam and my future. They were so caring. They made an appeal for finance for our superannuation. When I'd entered ministry way back in 1972, there was no such thing as enforced superannuation. What super I had accumulated had taken a massive hit with the financial crash of 2008. We will ever be grateful for the $42,000 given to our superannuation during this time.

As the money came in for this gift, it made all the more real that we were leaving YD. The numbness wasn't going, yet succession planning moved ahead with that whole bunch of friends I knew as 'the board'. They were helping me through it. They were brave in not allowing friendship to interfere with what was best for the kingdom. It's a bravery I will be ever grateful for. It's hard to tell a friend, 'It's time to go.'

The Preparing

I'm sitting in church minding my own business, listening to Chris Danes share one morning. As mentioned earlier, Chris was a much-loved former staff member. Ho hum, I think; he's preaching on Peter getting out of the boat. How many sermons have you heard on this story?

As I'm listening, Chris homes in on Peter saying, 'Lord if it's you, bid me come.' Then the application comes: 'What is the Lord bidding you to come to?' I think jokingly, 'Thanks for nothing, Chris!' But I could hear that the Lord was gently whispering, 'I'm calling you to come.' I think to myself, 'Okay Lord, I'm coming … coming out of YD to a new season.'

It was all part of the preparing.

Do you have anyone you have a text relationship with? You must! Geoff Shepherd has been my text buddy for years. We often send thoughts, ruminations and verses of Scripture to each other. Geoff sent me this verse as I was in a fog about my future: 'Jesus replied, "You don't understand now what I am doing, but some day you will"' (John 13:7, NLT). I often find the timing of thoughts sent by friends as vital as the actual thought itself. The timing was perfect – miraculous, even.

It was all part of the preparing.

He was at least a dozen years older than me and his name was Captain Rodger. He was a retired ship's captain who started out in the merchant navy from Scotland at the age of sixteen. I remember when I led a youth group in my early twenties, inviting him along to speak to our youth. I loved his heart for the gospel, and the youth seemed to respond to him. I admired how he invested his life in so many young people on a one-to-one basis. I admired how he coped with the loss of his dear wife when he was in his fifties.

I hadn't seen him for years, but we gradually struck up a friendship over my last ten years at YD. He was now in his eighties and still going strong for Jesus. We laughed and talked so easily together. I saw this guy as a gift from the Lord, showing me what one could do for the Lord while in retirement. He was amazing.

It was all part of the preparing.

There was much more the Lord did to prepare Pam and me for leaving YD ministry, but this is a sufficient tasting plate of the Lord's preparing.

Even the Son of God had a 'preparing'. John the Baptist prepared the way.

Isn't that exciting? If the Son of God had a 'preparing', then it makes sense that our loving Father has seasons of preparing for us. Sometimes it's preparing for entry; other times, it's preparing for moving on. I was discovering that the Lord was preparing me for the latter.

The Lord will watch over your coming and going
both now and forevermore.
Psalm 121:8 NIV

Walking in the Shadows

Ever had that sense of wishing someone you love could be with you to experience what you are seeing, feeling or doing? Pam and I have been blessed to go overseas a few times on trips to Europe. I can't imagine doing it by myself. We built memories together. I had someone I love with me. We would however, say sometimes, 'I wish (insert the name of one of our kids or grandkids) could see this.'

From 2012 on, until we walked out the door of YD in mid-2014, there were numerous times I had this wish. And the person I had in mind was Jesus. I knew he was with me, theologically, yet I wished that he was present with me in a way I could sense more tangibly. I desperately wanted him to speak to me in a 'loud' fashion, and it just wasn't happening. Ever felt that?

During this time, I was reading the book of Esther in conjunction with a Swindoll commentary. I noticed in this amazing book that the Lord's name is not once specifically mentioned. I also noticed that the Lord's hand is seen moving, on numerous occasions, without a word being spoken. He was there, but quietly orchestrating life from the shadows.

This verse from Psalms has a similar vibe: 'Your path led through the sea, your way through the mighty waters, though your footprints were not seen' (Ps 77:19 NIV). The Israelites walked through the Red Sea, but there was not even a gentle whisper of God's voice. Yet his presence was evident in the circumstance they found themselves in.

As the reality of leaving gradually hit me, I felt what can only be described as a numbness. I steeled myself for departure. Did this mess with my mind? Unbelievably. Listen to these diary entries:

> This week I have come face to face with leaving YD again. It seeps into my heart and sits there, damp and mouldy.

> Over the last few months I have suffered lapses, for apparently no reason, of melancholy. [One wonders how thick I could be not to work it out.]

At the same time, I was trying to lead in this numb state. Yet again, YD was in diabolical financial trouble. It seems the Lord wanted to keep us in a state of trust right until we walked out the door. In came a gift for $50,000.

Our schools work was starting to feel a deeper upfront opposition from school authorities and government rulings.

By the end of the year, staff now knew in reality that we were going, and it continued to unsettle some. Questions arose: 'Who will the board bring in? It doesn't seem obvious from within, so who? What will they be like? Will it impact my particular ministry?' The unsettledness was there beneath the surface, and it was growing.

In the middle of 2013, two of our staff, Sharon and Aaron, had, within days of each other, dreams that YD had demons posted around it. What was happening? Life at YD was going on and 'Mr Numb' was meant to be leading.

Do you know what encouraged me when I was desperate to hear the Lord's voice? It was the picture from the book of Esther of the Lord speaking through circumstances from the shadows. There was so much noise in my head I struggled to hear the garbage truck early Monday mornings, let alone Jesus. But this picture reminded me he was there.

If you are in a similar state trying to hear the Lord through overwhelming circumstances, be encouraged. Are you wishing someone who loves you were there with you? Jesus walks in the shadows. He loves you and he is there.

Who among you fears the Lord and obeys the word of his servant? Let the one who walks in the dark, who has no light, trust in the name of the Lord and rely on their God.
Isaiah 50:10 NIV

Managing or Leading?

What is the difference between a manager and a leader? Ask yourself, 'Am I managing or leading my home, my kids, my small group, my youth group, my congregation?'

At the beginning of 2013, we had twenty staff in YD. It sounds impressive, particularly when you realise all but two were on faith support, relying on God's people to provide their salary through regular personal giving. But only six were full time; the other fourteen were part time. A part-timer's hours could be as high as four days a week or as little as one day a week.

At the end of 2012, after some reflection, I had realised I'd been managing staff rather than leading them. I can see how, with the personal grief our family was feeling through the death of Pam's parents and the crisis of Adrian's journey, plus the grief of our time ending at YD, I had simply let maintaining the status quo become the way we functioned. I would manage staff pastoral issues where appropriate, manage finance as it raised challenges, manage the practical side of ministry by letting staff have their head, as long as it didn't rock the boat – and so it went on.

It was one of those pleasant, still evenings at the YD office. The air was still, the sun was setting and the familiar sounds of nature that emanate from a country property filled the air. All the staff had gone home. The year was almost finished. Pam and I sat on the wooden steps of YD's entrance and had one of those sweet moments. We knew the end of our ministry was in its sunset. We sat and reflected on all the Lord had blessed us with at YD. It was soothing, sitting there in the quietness of a summer rural setting. It was one of those thankful moments one can experience with Jesus. The end was near for us and we simply bathed in a moment of thankfulness.

But unfortunately, I was not leading.

Then, in this potpourri of gratitude, numbness and managing, I had a gradual reawakening, a return to being the visionary I should be. Out of this hot mudpool of emotions erupted a zeal I had not experienced for a long time. I can't explain it. I ask myself now, 'Why were you so zealous?' Surely as the end draws near, it's natural to taper off! I can only put it down to the Lord working miraculously in my heart. I was determined to change and lead, not manage.

What transpired? I prayed like I had never prayed before. I spent all of March 2013 in extended prayer. The Lord was taking hold of my heart's desires. I prayed for schools like I hadn't prayed in decades. The sense of the opportunity to share the gospel in schools was fading. I prayed fervently that the Lord would bring revival in schools. How good would it be if Christian students in schools had hearts burning for Jesus? What if students were set on fire for the Lord? How could the authority figures in schools and government resist this? I prayed for doors to open into Catholic schools. I poured out my heart for Healesville Secondary College, which had closed its doors on us. I called for staff to attend morning prayer meetings before the daily official YD work commenced.

This was not Rob trying hard to be spiritual. It was the Lord putting an enormous burden on my heart for schools. Why was the Lord doing this when my forty-three years of schools work was almost over? I don't know, but I had certainly moved out of managing and back to leading our staff. I was desperate for the vision to be reignited. These moments that were far more than manufactured moments of enthusiasm. I remember my old boss Bryan Greenwood saying, 'If the Lord gives you a burden to pray, never postpone it.'

Unknown Agendas

Let me digress for a moment from the YD story to tell you of some moments our youngest daughter, Nicole and husband, Adrian experienced. It will give context for what follows.

The bike accident that broke Adrian's back, leaving him needing a fistful of medication to survive, took its toll on them. Despite some amazing rehabilitation, Ade was unable to do more than a couple of days' work at a time before the pain would take him to a difficult place, making it impossible for him to keep going without a significant rest. My diary is littered with prayers for Ade as he contemplated his future.

Nicole was hit with a period of deep grief. She had had to be so strong with her kids, and with Adrian, while he recovered from his near-death experience. Ade now was coming to grips with what life might look like for him. It finally caught up with our Nic, too, and brought for her many sessions of quiet tears.

Pam and I prayed lots. You know those times when you feel so helpless with your kids, that nothing you do is going to help? How did we pray for her during this time? I asked God to lead Nic and Ade in his paths. I prayed for Nicole, 'Grant to her a special day where she will know your encouragement. Lord, continue to build into her a resilience, a strength to trust you when there seems no way forward.' Little did I know what I was praying for – but more about that later.

Nicole had an experience one night of Satan sitting on the end of her bed in a dark form. One wonders if he knew what was coming.

Despite all this pain for Nicole, she had some rather supernatural experiences. Here are two.

Nicole was walking home and saw a man yelling at his car. The engine was running and it was on a slope. Inside the car was a child in a car seat and a dog. The situation was urgent and dangerous; the car looked as if it could disappear down the slope at any moment. The dog had somehow walked over the console and had accidentally locked the car. The man was desperate to get in and couldn't. Nicole went over to the frantic man and prayed out loud, 'Jesus, open the door.' The door unlocked; the child was saved. The father and the boy were stunned by what happened. Even more amazingly, when they opened the door, the lock in the door was still in the lock position. Suck on that!

In the same year, Nicole was driving from Healesville and at Coldstream she came across a car crash. She went over to the car and there was an elderly couple who had crashed on the way to a birthday party. Nicole saw that the critically injured lady was in a bad way and in panic mode. Nicole started praying for the lady. Another passer-by saw this and thought Nicole was a loony, but Nicole kept praying. The injured lady passed away as Nicole was praying for her, but the panic had gone and peace had washed across her face before dying. (Nicole said she would have loved to have seen what was going on in heaven.) Nicole also felt the Lord was telling her to thank the police and fire folk attending for all they do. She told them how good they were in handling these repeated life-threatening situations. The man she talked to almost dissolved in tears.

Who knows why this all happened, but they were clearly 'God moments', with an agenda that only the Lord knows.

Never underestimate the random moments that God gives you. While we have not read the first or last pages of their life story, those random moments with strangers are a part of the story. We are to be a word, a paragraph or even a chapter in the book of their lives – but the Lord only knows how the story will end.

Closure

What I am about to write is for those of you who are wrestling with the process of bringing closure to a significant chapter in your life. The principle is the same, regardless of the story.

On Christmas eve of 2012, I wrote in my diary, 'The reality of leaving YD continues to sink in. I am so, so split down the centre, between a growing conviction this is right and a deep sadness that makes me feel incredibly lonely.'

As you go through my diary in this last full year of YD, you might think that my mind is scrambled, but it was my heart that struggled most.

I'm driving down the Hume highway listening to my son's songs and I feel like bursting into tears. I walk out of the morning chapel talk with staff and students each Tuesday and feel like crying. I'm talking to Sharon, one of our staff, about schools, and I get all emotional.

I wrote in my diary, 'I feel like a three-year-old standing on the beach, waiting for the tsunami to arrive.' And later in the year, 'Every night this week, I felt sad. I'M NOT SURE WHAT THIS IS ABOUT!'

A principle I now understand about significant closure in one's life is this: there will be grief. I look back and wonder how I didn't see the obvious signs of grief.

For me, it was an inward battle. Was I sad because I was losing my identity in our beloved ministry, YD? I asked myself this and rebuked myself heavily. My identity, I told myself, was in Jesus, not my ministry.

Amazing as it might seem to you, I beat myself up over feeling sad about leaving. I saw my sadness as evidence that I was finding my significance in ministry. I viewed it as a sign of sin or pride rather than a normal response to a big change. Consequently, I didn't allow myself to legitimately grieve. I had put myself in a theological box that only increased my grief. I did not recognise that closure is often accompanied by grief.

I find it revealing that at the start of the year I had sought the Lord greatly, asking him to draw Pam and me closer to himself. And indeed, he was doing this – through a painful time of grief and closure. The Lord can take closure and use it as an instrument to draw us closer to him. And the second half of this year was to break me, yet make me, in new ways.

Finding Elisha or Joshua

How do you find a replacement for someone when the answer isn't obvious? The approach at a YD board level was very pragmatic. Names had been put forward in November 2012 and we were urged to pray. I had been praying so long over this, it was a wonder I didn't get an angel come and tell me to shut up!

It was now the February 2013 board meeting. There was a call for any last names to be put forward, and a suggestion to narrow the list of candidates. We were urged once again to pray over the list.

In April, Dave Carne used the word 'liminality' to describe my position. I'd never heard of the word; it could have been a gelato flavour, for all I knew. He described it as 'the space in between.' For me, the space in between was knowing I was leaving but not knowing when I was going. It was a weird and frustrating experience. I was struggling with both uncertainty and grief, and I found the uncertainty to be destabilising in so many ways. It's like I was looking into a black abyss, about to jump, without knowing how far it was to the bottom.

By the June board meeting, someone had put the name of Michael, my son-in-law, forward among some others. At this stage, I didn't know if Michael and Kim were the Lord's choice. On the one hand, I was very wary of YD being guilty of nepotism. On the other hand, I was dead scared that, if Michael and Kim didn't get the call, they would be irreparably hurt. They were excited about the prospect of Michael taking the helm.

We had a fierce half-hour debate at this board meeting about whether Pam and I could talk the situation through with Michael and Kim. We wanted to be a sounding board for our kids while the board sought God's will on who would be the new CEO. The answer was a firm 'No' from the board. To avoid any charge of favouritism or nepotism, we were not to discuss the subject at all with them. We were gagged.

What followed for the next four months was one of the most difficult times in our family life. Our family is huge on communicating and talking. It was like we had gone down to the local zoo and selected the largest elephant, then planted it in our relationship with Michael and Kim. The elephant in the room was deliberately put there for integrity's sake. Yet it was extremely strange, awkward and infuriating to not be able to discuss the obvious with our kin.

I had a favourite old NIV Bible, which I'd lost. I prayed for the best part of three years, on and off, that the Lord would help me find it. In July of 2013 I found it, three years after I had lost it. It was in our church. As I was reading the Gospel of John, I noticed an old note I had pencilled in (I write in my Bible all the time and put dates next to verses). I had scribbled in the margin, next to John 14, 'Troubled about my walk and future.' The note was from years and years ago. The verse, of course, was, 'Do not let your hearts be troubled. Trust in God, and trust also in me' (John 14:1 NIV). It calmed my troubled heart. Isn't the Lord's timing fantastic?

I knew my struggle was evident to others when Pam put a simple note on my pillow: 'I love my hubby lots and lots.' She signed it 'Your wifey', with an X. Pam is not a note writer, so it became quite special to me. The Lord can use such simple acts of love to encourage us.

By August, all other possibilities for CEO had been eliminated and Michael and Kim were the only names on the list. Yet at this stage, the board didn't have a clear conviction about whom the Lord was calling . They were saying of Michael and Kim, 'It's not yes, and it's not no.' Another special board meeting was called. I sat in the room as a non-board member, in silence, and watched as the Lord moved the conversation from a 'no' to a 'yes' regarding Michael's appointment.

Pam and I were, by this stage, convinced that Michael was meant for the position. But we couldn't, and didn't, say anything. I imagine the board would have guessed what we felt. I was encouraged by this verse from Daniel: 'He changes times and seasons' (Dan 2:21aNIV).

There was, however, a desire from the board to be absolutely sure. After yet another interview – five in all! – Michael and Kim were formally offered the call to lead YD on October 12. They duly accepted. It was a unanimous 'yes' vote.

Dennis, our chairperson, rang me on that Saturday at 10:30 am to tell me of the decision. At 11 am, I was literally shaking. Pam and I drove from Doncaster Shopping Town to an orchard in Donvale to get some fruit. We drove in silence, holding an indescribable mixture of elation and grief. I was staggered by our reaction. I expected myself to be as excited as a 90-year-old mum hearing she was to become a first time grandma! I still did not realise I was suppressing my grief at leaving.

The whole process of finding YD's Elisha or Joshua was testament to the godliness of the board, who so diligently sought the Lord's will. It drove me crazy at times, but now I am so thankful they took their time until they fully discerned the Lord's will.

Prayer, integrity and perseverance were keys to finding our Elisha. I'll be forever grateful for these qualities in the board.

Drenched in Grace

Have you ever felt the overwhelming sense of God's grace drenching you? That moment when you are blown away by his goodness to you? How good is it?

A week before the board appointed Michael, I received an email forwarded onto me from Mandy Stark, a former staff member. She had received an email from a mutual friend, Claire Dexter, who was involved in mission work in central Australia, alongside her husband. Claire didn't have my email address. She had no idea about me leaving YD; in fact, I hadn't seen her in over thirty years.

She was driving across somewhere in central Australia and had a curious experience. She described it in an email to Mandy, asking Mandy to forward it on to me if she thought it was okay. Here it is:

> On the way home in the car we were listening to worship music and out of the blue I had a picture and had Rob Coyle on my heart – random!
>
> I saw a baton and a racetrack. I sensed that Rob was worried about handing the baton on; in fact, it was more than worry, it was fear that the baton would be dropped. But I believe that God said to me, not only will the baton NOT be dropped, but the one carrying it took off so fast there was fire in their wake.
>
> I also sensed that the baton carrier may be someone that Rob had not initially thought of, someone that he would not have readily chosen to hand the baton to, but that God was doing something new and out of the box.
>
> I believe that Rob is, will be, handing over the reins of leadership to someone and has some real concerns about them being up to the task. I think this picture means that they are more than able in God. In fact, they will be able to build on Rob's foundation and take Youth Dimension to places where Rob could never have imagined …

Isn't that unbelievable? With no idea of what Rob Coyle was up to, Claire had this picture arrive on the screen of her heart. The Lord didn't have to do this. It was pure grace, a 'love touch' from the Lord.

In my final twelve months of leading YD, I had immersed myself in the book of Revelation. I had read it through on numerous occasions but, to my shame, I had never dived into the big picture. I still don't fully get Revelation, but I love the mystery of it and the abiding principles that can rock one's world. During this time, this incredible book transported me into an eternal perspective on life. I, like many of us, had so easily fallen into the rhythm of time and retiring. Reading Revelation was another drenching in love.

During the August period leading up to the decision on a CEO, I had health issues. My blood pressure was through the roof and the doctor said my heart would wear out at the rate I was going. The doctors saw an irregularity in my heart, pointing to a potential aneurism, which could burst and kill me. Later I was cleared of this. Eventually, after the decision about Michael, my blood pressure came down: a final love touch.

> Even to your old age and grey hairs I am he,
> I am he who will sustain you.
> I have made you and I will carry you;
> I will strengthen you and I will rescue you.
>
> Isaiah 46:4 NIV

Friday Was the Darkest Day of My Life

We all sat out on our deck, celebrating the birthday of our eldest granddaughter, Ella. A bunch of the grandkids were doing the grandchild romp around Nana and Pa's backyard, while us adults looked on, enjoying the family vibe.

Family is huge for us. We have always been passionate about family.

A day or so after Ella's birthday celebration, we were in beautiful Palm Cove having our yearly week away in our tropical paradise. The phone rang, and I could tell by Pam's tone of voice that a threatening shadow was entering our lives.

Jemima, Adrian and Nicole's only daughter, was very sick. She had been admitted to hospital and put in an induced coma for two days. We immediately booked a flight home, leaving the next day. I honestly cannot recall a longer night in my life as we tossed and turned, bathed in terror. I voiced to Pam the unthinkable: 'We could lose her.'

We arrived in Melbourne early evening and went straight to the hospital. By now, Jamie and Janie had flown in from the Sunshine Coast, and the rest of us were gathered around Jemima and Adrian and Nicole. You could lift your hand up and snatch a fistful of dread from the air in the room. Grey was the best way to describe the appearance of Ade and Nic. They had all been praying with a desperation that defied understanding.

The next day, Friday, saw seven doctors and nurses file into a small anteroom to address us as a family, which included my sister Zayda, her husband David and daughter, Zayda,

I will never forget sitting in that room at the Monash Hospital. The doctor simply told us Jemima was gone. The groan of grief from family in the room was deep and audible. In a breath, our hearts as a family had been smashed to pieces. Nicole looked across the room and, staring the medical team in the eyes, thanked the doctors and nurses for all they had done.

Our beautiful blonde seven-year-old ray of sunshine, Jemima, had gone home to be with Jesus.

'Friday was the darkest day of my life', I later recorded in my journal.

The pastor of Adrian and Nicole's church arrived with his wife, and they were the Lord's hands and mouth of comfort. Ade and Nic went with the pastor and his wife into the hospital room where Jemima was, and sang Jemima's favourite song, *10,000 Reasons*. The hospital staff present were reduced to tears. In the darkest hour, the melody of triumph sounded.

I will never forget wrapping my arms around Nicole and Jamison (her oldest boy). We were on our knees in the hospital corridor. I was hurting and feeling so helpless, and all I could dribble out was, 'I love you.'

Jemima was diagnosed initially with meningitis. Later we received a call from the hospital to all come in for special medication, as there was something else they couldn't explain in her system.

There was no casket at Jemima's celebration service, as the coroner wanted to do an autopsy. Somehow, this just rubbed more lemon in a bleeding wound.

Earlier, Nicole had said, 'I don't want to bury Mima, because she won't have a wedding.' What do you say to that? Words are so inadequate in deep grief.

The celebration service saw over a thousand attend. Jemima loved lollies and bright colours, so the church was decked out like a seven-year-old's party. There were balloons everywhere and lollies of all types on trestle tables along the back of the church. Truly, it was a funeral service such as you have never seen.

Jemima Sunday Barton was eventually buried on a Monday. Adrian, Nicole, Pam and I carried her small pink coffin. It hurt. Yet our sense of victory echoed in the hours after, when we went to the chocolate factory just outside of Yarra Glen and had the kind of yummies that Jemima would have loved.

An outpouring of love followed. All kinds of amazing gifts were lavished on Adrian, Nicole, Jamison and Eli from church family. Donvale Christian College was very gracious in honouring and mourning Jemima as a student there. They had a minute's silence for Jemima at school and dedicated a garden area to her. Later on in April, they lined the school fence with helium balloons to celebrate her birthday. And they were very accommodating to Nicole, who was teaching part-time at the school.

For Pam and me, who are pretty private people, the tender care was poured out for us in waterfall proportions. The YD family were caring and completely understanding. I don't know how much I talked about our grief – knowing me, probably too much. They just took us into their hearts. Our own church, Heathmont Baptist, simply lavished us with practical support, along with prayer and comforting words. None of us wanted to cook, and for the first time I appreciated why the good old casserole is such a winner when a person is in grief. Lastly, Pam's sister Ruth was a quiet but effective comfort to her grieving sister.

What did I learn immediately from this tragic time? When you are numb from grief, Jesus bends down through his body and carries you. Sometimes, as a leader, you forget you need carrying or become too proud to be carried.

Angels

The Sunday before Jemima went down with meningitis, she was transfixed on the Vineyard Church stage in Mt Evelyn. She stood motionless, seemingly staring into nothing. Her cousin, Matilda, had tried to gain her attention, but there was no response. The other children waved ribbons as the church worshipped God. But she just stood there, finally saying, 'I love you, Jesus.' Later, when asked what had happened, she said, 'I saw angels.'

A couple of months before this, Jemima had gone into Nicole and Adrian's bedroom and said, 'There is an angel sitting on the end of my bed.'

What do you do with that? To my shame, I thought it a bit of a child's fantasy until the Lord led me to these verses:

> **See that you do not look down on one of these little ones,**
> **for I tell you that their angels in heaven always**
> **see the face of my Father in heaven.**
> Matthew 18:10 NLT

> **Are not all angels ministering spirits sent to serve those**
> **who will inherit salvation?**
> Hebrews 1:14 NIV

There were other verses the Lord gently led me to that brought me to one conclusion. Mima's experience was amazingly genuine. In fact, it was miraculous.

Ade and Nic went to church the Sunday after Jemima went to heaven. It was barely two days later. Nicole had read the passage in Scripture about David's grief after losing his son. He went and washed himself and worshipped. Nicole and Ade responded similarly. They were first down the front of church to worship that morning. People came to the Lord that day at church.

For our family, it knocked a proverbial hole in our collective heart, which the wind of grief still blows through to this present day.

For Pam, who loves like only a grandmother can love, it crushed her. She had been out on a special Jemima–Nan outing just before it all happened. Jemima, for a reason only the Lord knows, said to Pam while they were out,

'Nanny, I love you.'

I could see Pam's smashed heart. The Lord gave me this lovely verse to claim for her:

. **May the Lord, the God of Israel, under whose wings you have come to take refuge, reward you fully for what you have done.**

Ruth 2:12 NLT

Remember to keep praying for grieving people.

For me, the Lord laid on my heart that old hymn, *There were Ninety and Nine*, which tells the old story of the shepherd searching the hills for his lost sheep. I know Jemima wasn't lost, but I felt the Shepherd had come to take her home. I sang this as I drove home after taking Nicole back to Healesville days after the event. It tied in beautifully with a verse that was medicating my aching heart: 'He gathers the lambs in his arms and carries them close to his heart' (Isa 40:11b NIV). This sense of the Lord gathering our lamb Jemima and holding her close to his heart brought comfort to my soul.

This was another of those times I asked the Lord, 'Why?' It's always at a crossroads in our faith when that question raises its hand in our heart. There is nothing like grief to fertilise that question so that it rises from the earth of our heart and blossoms like a black rose. For Pam and me, Jemima was the exclamation mark on a season of grief. Leaving YD was a slow, seeping grief, while the death of Mima was a dam-busting sorrow.

Grief can possess you and take your eyes off Jesus. It's fascinating, when you're in danger of being completely possessed by sorrow, what the Lord can bring across your path. I read a quote of Robert Murray Mc Cheynne, who said, 'For every one look at myself, I look ten times at you, Lord Jesus.'

I had to learn to practise looking at Jesus rather than opening gates in my mind that would lead down a dark alley of looking at the circumstances that paralysed me with grief. I know many of you reading this will have faced that choice too. It's so hard.

Awkward

What makes you cringe inside? What makes you say, 'Awkward – I want out of here?' What makes you blush so hard that you can't hide it? It's the kind of feeling that most of us dislike so much, we will do everything in our power to avoid it.

I felt this feeling washing over my heart as Wendy, my faithful serving secretary, started to make preparations for my YD farewell. Pam and I would rather wrestle a dozen malnourished crocodiles than face what was coming. We cringed inside at the thought of not only a farewell dinner but a farewell family afternoon and service.

Poor old Wendy bore the brunt of my quiet resistance. Wendy and a team of others were pulled together to run these events. Finally, the Lord knocked sense into me like a blow to the head with a cement clothes hoist. I was not giving people who had stood with us, over many years, the opportunity to rejoice in what the Lord had done through us. The farewell was not about us but about the Lord's faithfulness over many years.

We look back now and have a deep appreciation for all Wendy and company put into making our final farewell weekend such a great celebration.

When you've lived by people's faithful financial and prayerful support over a period of forty-three years, there grows in you an unfathomable gratitude for every prayer offered and every cent given. God's people, moved by him, had worked hand-in-hand with us to reach literally thousands of young people with the gospel. Words cannot describe our thankfulness for this persistent care over so long.

In the early months of 2014, we struggled in the lead up to leaving. Around mid-March, however, we embraced it with thankful hearts. Again, Scripture ministered to us. Early in the year, I read, 'The Lord will watch over your coming and going both now and forevermore' (Psalm 121:8 NIV). Apparently in the original text, it puts 'going' before 'coming'. We certainly were going first, before coming to what the Lord had for us next.

The Friday farewell dinner, in June 2104, saw ex-board and staff members come with their partners. It felt like a time warp, with Eric Price, our first chairperson, and many other familiar faces from our history, present with us. I simply shared a short thought on Paul's words: 'Finally brothers, farewell.'

The Saturday afternoon family time saw the whole of the YD staff put in an enormous effort, with all kinds of fun activities. It was a hoot.

The final service, on the Saturday evening, was full of laughs and gratitude to the Lord for all he had done. Each of our children spoke, which was so encouraging. So many children of parents in ministry disappear over the horizon, never to be seen again. Each of our children and their partners has made the choice to stay close to the heart of Jesus. This is God's grace to us and a reflection of their hearts and choices rather than any brilliant parenting on our part.

I had the opportunity to respond to all the lovely events of the day. I can't remember what I said, but I do recall being engulfed by a tidal wave of emotion. These kind folk stood and applauded at the end of my expression of thanks. So many of these people, whom the Lord raised up to carry us in ministry, were not just expressing an appreciation for us but also for the Lord's faithfulness to an ordinary couple.

God uses ordinary people.

At the end of the evening, Michael and Kim were commissioned by Ross Grace, a long-serving board member and dear friend, on behalf of us all. A number of objects were given to Michael to signify the elements of his ministry and life for the future. Among these was a baton. I found it so meaningful in the light of Claire Dexter's prophetic email.

'I Walked in with Dad and I Walked out with Dad'

The last day of thirty-six years in the one job has to be ... pick a word!

As was traditional with every exiting staff member, we had been out for a celebratory lunch. It was eerie watching those last hours tick over.

There had been many 'lasts' during the week: the last time in a school, the last staff meeting, the last chapel service with the whole student body. There was the last one-to-one with Paulie Bremner, whom I had met up with fortnightly for eight years. From the time he came to us as an eighteen-year-old, I've loved Paulie's heart for the Lord.

The lasts rolled on until it was the last minute.

I stood at the YD entrance door and said goodbye as each staff person walked out. As you would have guessed, the tears quietly flowed.

Over the years, the Lord has given YD a great many staff. I am unashamed to say that I loved them. Up there with sharing the gospel with teenagers was the thorough enjoyment I experienced in sharing fellowship with my staff family over so many years. Although many have not received a mention in this book, each one has had a part of my heart. As with any family, there were rocky moments, but each person contributed towards the making of YD and the moulding of my own character.

What can I say in gratitude for all the unknown prayers offered up for us Coyles? We've had people pray for us every day for years. Some have prayed once, others faithfully over the long term. We are grateful for every treasured prayer offered. It has carried us as a family. Then there are the monetary gifts of God's people, some one-off, others through consistent giving over decades, and every cent a gift from the Lord's hand as he stirred the hearts of his children. It is humbling to be on the receiving end.

And what about family? What can I say of the kids? This includes of course their partners, whom we have always viewed as our kids, too. And the grandkids? Words stick in my throat as I try to inadequately express our gratitude to them. In the latter years, after my own Mum's passing, we have loved getting closer to my sister Zayda, her husband David and their lovely daughter, another Zayda (whom I call 'Zaydes'). They have become family to us in a new way and have stood by us without so much as blinking. Their loyalty has been unstinting.

As we headed for the last time to our car, the Lord granted me one last blessing: a magnificent, divinely painted sunset. I had prayed for one. Michael, Pam and I stood in the evening solitude of the YD grounds. All the staff had gone by now. I picked up my computer, then Michael drove us home. Pam sent a text to Jamie, our son: 'I walked in with Dad and I walked out with Dad.'

How can I acknowledge in writing the blessing of having Pam by my side? She has been as such a pillar of support in life and ministry. No one but I will know how deep and how profound having the backing of this little five-foot-two inches of a lady has been. She was, and always will be, God's gift to me.

When people think of miracles, the natural inclination is to picture the unbelievable – walking on water, incredible healings or the raising of the dead. All of these are very possible. We saw a few amazing miracles in our time, but we saw many more of what we would call 'ordinary' miracles: miracles of provision, of life change, of new spiritual birth, of relational healing, of timely verses or events, of divine guidance. They were not necessarily show stopping, but they were such that could only be described as God's doing. Isn't that the very definition of a miracle?

As these memories should convince you, we are just ordinary people who experienced many ordinary miracles. The Lord's faithfulness to us is beyond measure. Without any hint of plastic spirituality, we recognise the Lord has done it all and we have, along with many others, been ordinary tools in his hands.

Acknowledgements

There are many folk who have marked Pam and my lives but who are not mentioned in this book. We are forever grateful for them. The Lord knows who they are. They will receive their reward in heaven, rather than in this little book of reflection!

Epilogue

Pam and I had our wedding reception in Healesville, a small country town on the outskirts of Melbourne. Pam, who had lived on a farm not far from Healesville, had told me on numerous occasions, 'I'll never live in the country again.'

It's 2017 and we are having some renovations done on our house by a lovely Christian builder. He drops it to us that the LORD had caused him to sell his house he had lived in for 6 months to go to Healesville. In the process he bought a block of land. The seller accidentally sold him two blocks for one!

He joked we might like to buy it and build there. What, at 73? No way! Besides Pam hates the country. Our daughter and son-in-law who run a church there started to tease us about coming up. Funny, but no way.

One day Pam says, 'I wouldn't mind living in Healesville.' My reply was, 'What!' To cut a long story short, I had an argument with the LORD until He stamped on my heart. 'Go.'

Seasons never stop, do they?

Michael's season as leader of YD came to an end after he had done the difficult job of bringing transition about. He is now in church pastoral ministry. Another season change. Jamie and Janie (our son and daughter-in-law) moved out of evangelism with their band, Selaphonic, to pastoring a Hillsong Church in Noosa. Another season change.

YD now has Lindsay Tundbridge heading it up with re-entry into schools and re-igniting summer mission outreach. It's so exciting to see the LORD opening new doors. Another season change.

This book has been 15 years in the making and so much has happened. The road has been littered not only with change, but oh so many ordinary miracles. I trust that in whatever season you find yourself, you will find the same LORD doing the ordinary miracles in your life.

Every blessing,
Rob

www.ingramcontent.com/pod-product-compliance
Lightning Source LLC
La Vergne TN
LVHW051412080426
835508LV00022B/3050